Steve and Jannie's Home Cookin' Recipes

Also by Janice Lynn Ross

Crepes and Coyotes and Other Tales:
The Companion Book to Steve and Jannie's
Home Cookin' Recipes

Like Water from a Spring:
Poems, Stories, Reflections, and Pencil
Scratches from a Long-Forgotten Box

Steve and Jannie's Home Cookin' Recipes

≈≈≈≈≈≈≈≈≈

Janice Lynn Ross

Copyright © 2019 by Janice Lynn Ross
All rights reserved

Cover photograph by Janice Lynn Ross
Photograph of author by John Morefield

ISBN 978-1-7105-8253-6

www.amazon.com/author/janicelynnross

*With love
to my husband, Steve.*

*Thank you
for your love, support, and patience;
for sharing your recipes;
for cooking delicious meals.*

*Without you, this book would not exist.
You are the inspiration of,
and cooking talent behind,
this book.*

*Let's be grateful
on a daily basis
for access
to clean water
and healthy food.*

Janice Lynn Ross

Cookbook Sections

Chicken-in-a-Pot............1

Soups..................….......6

Salads.............…......…36

Poultry.....................…..62

Pork....….................…..81

Beef......…..............…...94

Warm Vegetables…......109

This and That..…..........121

Desserts..............…....141

Quick Bread...…….......150

Smoothies.................163

Breakfasts…....….........169

Contents

Introduction: I Flunked High School Cooking Class i

CHICKEN-IN-A-POT
In the Beginning There Was Chicken-in-a-Pot 2
Chicken-in-a-Pot 3
After Chicken-in-a-Pot 4

SOUPS
Variety and Deliciousness Achieved Simply 7
Real Chicken Soup 8
Steve's Spicy Hot Chicken Soup 9
The Perfect Recipe 10
Juanita's Spicy Chicken Soup 11
Cooking for Yourself 12
Magic Minestrone 13
Montana Hot and Sour Soup 14
Quick Chicken Soup 15
Tomato Vegetable Stew 16
Shelly's Borscht 17
Classic Lentil Soup 18
Lentil Soup with Sun-Dried Tomatoes 19
Lentil Soup with Tomatoes 20
Irene's Split Pea Soup 21
Steve's Split Pea Soup 22
Noe Valley Corn Chowder 23
Shrimp in Corn Chowder 24

Veggies in Vegetable Broth 25

Stovetop Pot of Beans 26

How Much Seasonings to Use? 27

Ham and Bean Soup 28

Vegetarian Bean Soup 29

Potato Leek Soup in Amsterdam 30

Amsterdam Potato Leek Soup with Beer 31

Vegan Potato Leek Soup with Beer 32

Susanne's Ravioli Soup 33

Big Timber Hamburger Soup 34

Capture the Liquid 35

SALADS

Carrot Broccoli Salad 37

Steve's Favorite Potato Salad 38

Various Versions of Potato Salad 39

Curry Potato Salad 40

O & V Bleu Cheese Crumbles Potato Salad 41

J&S Macaroni Salad 42

Mediterranean Pasta Salad 43

Sherry's Spaghetti Salad 44

Shrimp Parmesan Orzo Salad 45

Chicken Parmesan Orzo Salad 46

Tahini Salad Dressing 47

Citrus Sesame Oil Salad Dressing 48

Deluxe Salad 49

Maple Mustard Salad Dressing 50

Three Sisters Salad 51

Three Sisters and a Brother Salad 51

St. Patrick's Day Salad Dressing and Salad 52

Jannie's Creamy Yogurt Salad Dressing 53

Chris's California Salad..54

Loretta's Salad 55

Thousand Island Salad Dressing...56

Steve's Coleslaw 57

In-a-Hurry-No-Refrigerator-Needed Coleslaw 58

Coleslaw with Salsa 59

River Bean Salad 60

Bean and Corn Salad 61

POULTRY

Turkey Spaghetti...63

An Easier Tomorrow—Having Inventory 64

Creamy Chicken Casserole 65

Stefano's Easy Chicken Cacciatore 66

Chicken Cordon Blue-Eyed Steve 67

Chicken Baked in Steve's BBQ Sauce 68

Steve's BBQ Sauce for Baking...69

Curry Chicken Strips 70

Do You Like that Rock?...71

Rosemary Coriander Chicken...72

Chicken Fried Rice 73

Chicken with Vegetables over Rice..74

Curry Chicken with Vegetables over Rice 75

Spicy Cornflake Chicken Bites...76

Paprika Chicken..77

Cinnamon & Cumin Chicken 78

Chicken Enchilada Casserole 79

Steve's Moist Herbed Thanksgiving Turkey 80

PORK

Sweet and Sour Pork over Rice 82

Verde Valley Pork Verde 83

Chicken in Pork Verde Broth 84

Boneless Country Ribs, Marinated and Baked 85

Boneless Country Ribs, Parboiled and Baked 86

Steve's BBQ Sauce for Baking 87

Steve's Pork Roast 88

Steve's Marinade for Pork 89

Pork Roast with Fruit 90

Pork Fried Rice 91

Pork with Vegetables over Rice 92

Curry Pork with Vegetables over Rice 93

BEEF

California Pot Roast 95

Steve's Beef Stew (in a Slow Cooker) 97

Steve's Marinade for Beef Stew and Chili 98

What is Chili? 99

Steve's Beef Chili (in a Slow Cooker) 100

Beef Chili Vegetable Soup 101

Seasoned Ground Beef 102

Steve's Favorite School Lunch 104

Our Down-home Meatloaf 105

Swedish Meatballs 106

Shepherd's Pie 107

Beef Enchilada Casserole 108

WARM VEGETABLES

Byron's Brussels Sprouts 110
Warm German-American Potatoes 111
A Potato for Dawn 112
Scrumptious Scalloped Potatoes 113
Skillet Eggplant with Zucchini and Mushrooms 114
Skillet Eggplant with Tomatoes 115
Cauliflower with Red Bell Pepper 116
Honey Glazed Carrots 117
Katy's Kale 118
Collard Greens 119
Curry Vegetables 120

THIS AND THAT

Great Guacamole 122
Esteban's Salsa Verde 123
Quesadillas and Soft Tacos 124
Pigs in a Serape 125
Thai Pizza 126
Sautéed Shrimp over Rice 127
Joey's Marinara Sauce 128
Spaghetti Stretcher 129
Vegetables in Mild Marinara Sauce 130
Darla's Pasta Primavera 131
Steve's Three-Cheese Lasagna 132
Paula's Party Dip 133
S & J's Deviled Eggs 134
The Veggieloaf 135

Broccoli and Mushroom Veggieloaf 136

Chicken Salad Sandwiches 137

Curry Chicken Salad Sandwiches.. 138

Tuna Salad Sandwiches 139

Fried Tofu 140

DESSERTS

Raisin Cornmeal Custard 142

Apple Raisin Rice Custard... 143

Creamy Lemon Pie 144

New Fairy Cookies 145

Cocoa Cake 146

Pear and Apple Crisp 147

Pear and Blackberry Crisp 148

Anytime Skillet Apples... 149

QUICK BREAD

A Grand Variety of Quick Breads 151

Jannie's Basic Quick Bread 153

It's a Meditation... 154

Hippie Quick Bread 155

Cinnamon Apple Raisin Quick Bread 156

Orange Juice Apple Quick Bread 157

Nutmeg Fruit Quick Bread 158

Exuberance Quick Bread 159

Honey Bran Raisin Muffins... 160

Corn Muffins 161

Mixed Fruit Muffins 162

SMOOTHIES

Smoothie Talk 164

Fruit Smoothies 165

Cocoa Smoothie 168

BREAKFASTS

Slim Breakfast Casserole 170

Fried Cornmeal Mush 171

Jannie's Home-fried Potatoes 172

Home-fries for Dawn 173

Gringo Huevos Rancheros 174

Steve's Breakfast Special 175

Yogurt and Fruit 176

San Francisco Granola 177

Allspice Benvenue Pancakes 178

Buckwheat Pancakes 179

Pancakes for One 180

Cinnamon Syrup 181

Crepes 182

Berry Syrup 183

Blintzes (Filling for Crepes) 184

Lessons Learned 185

Acknowledgements 186

About the Author 188

Introduction: I Flunked High School Cooking Class

I *tried* following the recipes in cooking class, but my group and I bombed, repeatedly. Our cooking creations were lessons in what *not* to do. Our sauce was lumpy. Our pie filling was soupy. Our cake fell. How humiliating in front of the other girls. I was mortified that I failed the cooking unit of my high school homemaking class.

Hey, out of failure comes success, right? It's the phoenix concept: out of the ashes of a fire rises a beautiful bird who soars to new heights. *You* know that when you fail it just motivates you to double down and try harder to succeed, to get it right. In fact, if I hadn't failed that cooking class, maybe I wouldn't be so enthusiastically cooking today.

Actually, things were better than I realized. My mom, Dee, gave us four kids (Jean, Brian, June, and I) a firm foundation in nutrition—serving our family balanced meals, using a wide variety of fruits, vegetables, and whole grains. We kids learned from her how to select fresh produce and other items at the grocery store. This knowledge has served us well as adults. She also—very consistently—cooked our breakfasts, packed our lunches, and got dinner on the table. Quite a feat, quite a role model. (My mom, by the way, is 93 years old and just returned from a beautiful six-week road trip with June through Canada and Alaska.)

It wasn't till I set out on my own, though, that I blossomed as a cook. I learned from my peers, and I will tell you a little bit about some of them:

- In Isla Vista, California—in our very first away-from-home apartment—my college friend Roberta showed me how she made casseroles. We were nineteen.

- In the soggy Northwest, while taking a break from college, housemates Joey, Naomi, and Ann taught me some valuable cooking skills. Joey showed me how to make Italian marinara sauce and whole grain yeast bread. Naomi showed me how to pick berries and bake fruit pies. Ann showed me how to bake quick breads.

- In Berkeley, housemate Carolyn showed me how to brew coffee starting with grinding whole beans. She also taught me how to bake a cocoa cake. From housemates Greg and Randy I learned that real men do in fact cook. (Also learned from Greg to warm my hands over the toaster while waiting for bread to toast.)

- In San Francisco, in the shadow of Twin Peaks, boyfriend Eric showed me how to create soups, chowders, and calamari. Girlfriends Chris and Paula knew all about presentation—how to make it look appetizing.

    I would not be the person I am today had these people, and others, not shown me what they knew.

    We were fearless; there was nothing we wouldn't try cooking. We cooked at home for economic reasons, yes, but also because we wanted to eat delicious, nutritious food, and the best way to do that was to make it ourselves. Creativity played a role, as well. We enjoyed creating our dishes, working out the recipes, taking note what to change next time. And being creative—in whatever endeavor you choose—is always a good thing!

Chicken-in-a-Pot

In the Beginning There Was Chicken-in-a-Pot

In Montana, one Sunday evening in June 2014, I received an email from my brother, Brian, which simply read "Send me your soup recipes." I love my brother's succinctness—no wasted words, no wasted time, just right to the point.

My first thought was, I'll send him Steve's *Real Chicken Soup* recipe. But I quickly realized I couldn't do that without first providing his *Chicken-in-a-Pot* recipe. So I asked my husband how he made that, typed up both recipes, and hit "send" that same evening. Okay, I thought, I'm done. But something took root that evening and I've never been quite the same since.

Two things. First, I was *curious* how my husband actually created his delicious dishes and so, as he cooked, I began hovering over him—asking questions and writing it all down.

Second, I wanted to *share* Steve's recipes, as well as my own, with family, and so I created, in binder-style, a 40-recipe book, *Cooking in Montana*. I named it that because we spent much of our time, well, *cooking*. Wintertime was like being on another planet—dangerously icy, snowy, and cold—and on weekends we often stayed home and cooked. Then July would come 'round and we were back on planet Earth, flinging open doors and windows—still cooking, cooking, cooking—on the days we weren't out fishing, boating, rock collecting, or sightseeing.

So *that* was how all of *this* began. Since the evening of Brian's email, we have circled the sun five times, Steve and I now call Florida home, and here is a much bigger cookbook. Whenever possible, I tried to write small recipes, as if two people were eating together. When that was not possible, consider the leftovers as *inventory* (Steve's word)—convenient food to be enjoyed later!

Chicken-in-a-Pot
(aka Chicken Stew)

Slow cooked chicken, simmering in chicken broth. Simple and nourishing, Chicken-in-a-Pot *is a Sunday favorite, the start of many good things. From this wholesome dish you save the leftovers for a variety of other dishes on future days. Steve says, "Stewed chicken is an ancient dish. As long as people have had a cooking pot, they've been making* Chicken-in-a-Pot.*"*

1 whole chicken, 4 to 6 lbs
14 oz (1 can) chicken broth
14 oz water
1 cup white wine
1/4 cup olive oil
3 carrots (dice 2, slice 1)
3 celery stalks (dice 2, slice 1)
A carbohydrate, "carb": rice, egg noodles, cubed potatoes, etc.

1 medium onion, chopped
2 tsps curry powder
2 tsps Poultry Seasoning
Salt, to taste
Black pepper, to taste

- Get an extra-large pot with a lid and add in: whole chicken (breast side to the top), broth, water, wine, oil, *diced* carrot, *diced* celery, onions, and seasonings. Bring to a boil. Reduce heat to low (gentle bubble). Cook, covered, 90 minutes.
- Meanwhile, cook your "carb" separately. Set aside.
- At the 80-minute mark, put the *sliced* carrot and celery in the pot. Cook, covered, on low, about 10 minutes.
- When the chicken is done, lift it out of the pot, place it in a shallow baking dish, and cut off pieces.
- Serve in individual bowls: spoon in carb, ladle in broth and veggies, and add in chicken pieces.

Serves 6.

Note: Steve says it's okay if your chicken sticks up a little through the liquid. It will steam (cook) as long as there's a lid on the pot.

After Chicken-in-a-Pot

You've cooked and eaten Chicken-in-a-Pot. *Fabulous! With the leftovers you are assured of additional delicious meals. Read on!*

Leftovers are a good thing. It means *inventory* ☺. It means easy cooking tomorrow. Less time and effort cooking—more time and enjoyment eating.

After dinner, this is what Steve does:

1. He takes the leftover chicken and *de-bones* it—a messy job but Steve says that by getting rid of the gristle, skin, and bone, your future dishes will look nicer and taste better.

2. Next he stores the chicken stock for future chicken soup.
   - He pours broth and vegetables from the large pot through a strainer. Then he pours the broth into 2 or 3 Pyrex containers.
   - He adds in chicken pieces to some containers. (You may prefer to keep all of the chicken separate and out of the broth.)
   - He labels and dates the containers and then places 1 or 2 in the refrigerator and 1 or 2 in the freezer.

3. Finally, he places the remaining de-boned chicken pieces in gallon-size freezer baggies, and labels and dates them. He stores one baggie in the refrigerator, the rest in the freezer.

Now it's all set for future meals! Recipes using leftover *Chicken-in-a-Pot* are in this cookbook:

Soup Section
- Real Chicken Soup
- Steve's Spicy Hot Chicken Soup
- Juanita's Spicy Chicken Soup
- Simple Minestrone
- Montana Hot and Sour Soup
- Lentil Soup
- Split Pea Soup
- Pot of Beans

Salad Section
- Add chicken to Sherry's Spaghetti Salad
- Chicken Parmesan Orzo Salad
- Deluxe Salad

Poultry Section
- Creamy Chicken Casserole
- Chicken Fried Rice
- Chicken Enchilada Casserole

Warm Vegetables Section
- A Potato for Dawn

This and That Section
- Quesadillas and Soft Tacos
- Thai Pizza
- Add chicken to Joey's Marinara
- Add chicken to Darla's Pasta Primavera
- Chicken Salad Sandwiches

Breakfast Section
- Add chicken to Slim Breakfast Casserole

This is so exciting! I hope you buy a whole chicken and create your own *Chicken-in-a-Pot* real soon!

Soups

Variety and Deliciousness Achieved Simply

The next five recipes use leftover *Chicken-in-a-Pot* stock. What you do is take your leftover *Chicken-in-a-Pot*, throw in a few other ingredients and, within minutes, *voila*—you've got a great soup to enjoy. Variety and deliciousness achieved simply.

A few words about the soup ingredients:

- You're going to see big lists of veggies in the recipes. Simply choose a few. Each time you cook soup, it can be different from the time before.

- "Carbs" (rice, pasta, potatoes) in your soup are optional.

- You may prefer a "carb" on the side (bread, tortillas) rather than in your soup.

- When using kale, collards, or mustard greens, dice them up, so they'll cook quicker.

- When using eggplant, give eggplant cubes a saltwater soak for at least 20 minutes to remove bitterness. More info in the *Skillet Eggplant with Zucchini and Mushrooms* recipe, Warm Vegetables section.

- Spices and herbs lose their potency over time. When that happens, I toss the bottle and replace it with a fresh one.

Real Chicken Soup
(Made from Leftover Chicken-in-a-Pot)

There is a magical quality about chicken soup—it soothes us, some say it can even heal us. With this recipe, you are working with leftover broth and chicken from previously-made Chicken-in-a-Pot. *No seasonings needed because they're already in the broth. Your troubles begin to melt away as soon as the broth begins to bubble! Just takes a few minutes to prepare. As for the big veggie list, simply choose a few.*

2 cups leftover *Chicken-in-a-Pot* (that is, chicken stock with or without chicken pieces)
An optional "carb": rice, egg noodles, cubed potatoes, etc.

1½ to 2 cups of vegetables, several kinds, cut up, such as:

green beans	lima beans	broccoli	celery
mushrooms	tomatoes	hominy	chard
beet greens	eggplant	parsley	corn
cauliflower	zucchini	carrot	peas

1/4 cup shredded cheese, as topping. Parmesan is good.

➢ Take your leftover *Chicken-in-a-Pot* from the freezer or refrigerator and skim off most of the fat (optional step).
➢ Cook your "carb." Set it aside when done.
➢ Put your leftover *Chicken-in-a-Pot* and raw vegetables into a soup pot.
➢ Bring to a boil, then reduce heat to low (barely bubbling) and cook, covered, until the veggies are done, about 10 minutes.
➢ To serve, scoop your "carb" into individual bowls, then ladle in the soup.
➢ Top with cheese.

Serves 3.

Steve's Spicy Hot Chicken Soup

Notice the big list of vegetables. Just choose a few, starting with whatever you have on hand.

2 cups leftover Chicken-in-a-Pot (chicken stock with or without chicken)
1 Tbsp olive oil

1½ to 2 cups of vegetables, several kinds, cut up, such as:

cabbage	green beans	tomatoes
carrot	mushrooms	parsley
celery	lima beans	onion
corn (or hominy)	eggplant	peas

1 Tbsp lemon or lime juice
Jalapeño: 4 to 8 diced jalapeño rings, from a jar *or*
     1/4 to 1/2 fresh jalapeño*, minced and de-seeded
Sriracha hot chili sauce, to taste
Seasonings, to taste, such as: chili powder, cumin, cayenne
1/4 cup shredded cheese, as topping

➢ Take your leftover *Chicken-in-a-Pot* from the freezer or refrigerator and skim off most of the fat (optional step).
➢ Put a tablespoon of olive oil into a soup pot. Add vegetables and cook over medium heat, about 3 minutes, stirring frequently.
➢ Add in leftover *Chicken-in-a-Pot* and lemon juice, jalapeño, hot sauce, and seasonings. Bring to a boil then lower heat to medium-low (barely bubbling) and cook for a few minutes, until vegetables are done.
➢ Ladle soup into bowls. Top with shredded cheese.

Serves 2 or 3.

Note: *Steve says some fresh jalapeños are like candy, others are hot, and that you have to taste it to know how much to use.

The Perfect Recipe

When I worked in San Francisco, I used to sneak out of the office, take the elevator down to the plaza, and head over to The Perfect Recipe. Heady aromas would greet me as I stepped into this café: a mysterious mixture of coffee, vanilla, herbs, and who knows what else. One secret afternoon, while I was furtively sipping a cappuccino there, a news crew came in. They talked with the manager and then approached me. They wanted to interview and film me while I was drinking my espresso and foamy milk. I couldn't let them do that! It might blow my cover! We compromised: they would film only my cappuccino and my hand, no interview.

In addition to coffee drinks, The Perfect Recipe also served soups. The minestrone was their best soup, in my opinion. But you know what? It wasn't always perfect. Neither were the cappuccinos.

As far as "perfect recipes" go, I don't believe in them. What tastes perfect to one person is far from perfect to another. We differ in our taste and texture preferences. Also, our moods affect our liking for certain ingredients and styles of cooking, so that one day something might taste delicious and another day it might taste yucky.

This brings me to the point of my missive: *There is no universal perfect recipe.*

With this cookbook, you will like some of the recipes, but you will not like all of them. You are your own person, and you have your own ideas about what tastes good and what does not. While it is true that we have carefully tested these recipes and personally like them, Steve and I suggest you use them as inspiration to create your own. Omit an ingredient, add in another one, or cook things in a different way. Do your own thing! Make it perfect for you!

Juanita's Spicy Chicken Soup

Notice the big list of vegetables. Just choose a few, starting with whatever you have on hand.

2 cups leftover *Chicken-in-a-Pot* (chicken stock with or without chicken)
1 Tbsp olive oil
1½ to 2 cups of vegetables, several kinds, cut up, such as:

mustard greens	beet greens	zucchini	carrot
yellow squash	cauliflower	spinach	celery
green beans	lima beans	hominy	corn
mushrooms	tomatoes	parsley	peas
bell pepper	eggplant	onion	kale

1/4 to 1/2 cup salsa*
1/4 cup shredded cheese, as topping

- Take your leftover *Chicken-in-a-Pot* from the freezer or refrigerator and skim off most of the fat (optional step).
- Put a tablespoon of olive oil into a soup pot. Add in vegetables and cook over medium heat, about 3 minutes, stirring frequently.
- Add in leftover *Chicken-in-a-Pot* and salsa. Bring to a boil then lower heat to medium-low (barely bubbling) and cook for a few minutes, until vegetables are done.
- Ladle soup into bowls. Top with shredded cheese.

Serves 2 or 3.

Notes:
*I prefer salsa from the *refrigerated* section of the grocery store.
*The amount of salsa to use depends on how spicy-hot the salsa is and how spicy-hot you like your food.

Cooking for Yourself

- "I rarely cook for myself. It's too much work and I don't have the time."

- "I'm tired when I get home from work; I don't have the energy to cook."

- "I cooked when the kids lived at home, but not much anymore. Why bother?"

- "I cooked when _____ was in my life. Now it's just me and I don't feel like cooking for myself."

You've heard those comments before. I've said some of those things, even cried over some of those words. Honestly, if I lived alone, I would not cook as much as I do now. Not as much, but I would still cook, just as I did during those many years I was single. Why? Cooking is fun and satisfying, and I like to eat good food!

Here's what I've learned from Steve: Spend some time and effort cooking, eat some now, and refrigerate or freeze some of it for later. Comes the day you don't feel like cooking, you just look in your "icebox" and pull out a delicious meal to heat up. *Inventory*. Can't count the number of times this has come in handy.

Magic Minestrone

Magic because it's so quick and easy. It's simply Real Chicken Soup *with pasta, Italian spices, tomatoes, and beans. (Notice the big list of vegetables. Just choose a few.)*

2 cups leftover Chicken-in-a-Pot (chicken stock with or without chicken)
1/4 cup uncooked Ditalini (or any shape pasta you like)
1 tsp canola oil
1/4 tsp Italian Seasonings
1 cup canned whole *or* diced tomatoes
1 cup canned beans (kidney, white, green, or garbanzo)

1½ to 2 cups of vegetables, several kinds, cut up, such as:

green beans	beet greens	zucchini	carrot
mushrooms	lima beans	broccoli	celery
bell pepper	tomatoes	chard	corn
cauliflower	eggplant	onion	peas

1/4 cup shredded cheese, as topping

➤ Skim off fat from your leftover *Chicken-in-a-Pot*.
➤ Cook pasta according to the directions on the package. When done, drain and stir in a teaspoon of oil. Set aside.
➤ Into a soup pot: leftover *Chicken-in-a-Pot*, seasonings, canned tomatoes, beans. Bring to a boil. Reduce heat to low. Cook, covered, 10 minutes.
➤ Add in vegetables. Cook, covered, on low, about 10 minutes.
➤ To serve, spoon pasta into individual bowls, ladle in soup. Top with cheese.

Serves 3.

Note: This recipe is very flexible: use more or less tomatoes, beans, and/or vegetables to suit your personal taste.

Montana Hot and Sour Soup

This is our version of Chinese hot and sour soup, concocted one Montana winter day when we didn't want to risk driving ten icy miles into town to eat hot and sour soup—although it was tempting. (Choose a few vegetables from this big list.)

1/8 lb pork (1 thin pork chop), thinly sliced
1 Tbsp soy sauce
2 Tbsps chopped onion and 1 Tbsp olive oil
2 cups chicken stock: one 14 oz can chicken broth
     ***or** leftover Chicken-in-a-Pot, with or without chicken*
2 Tbsps (or more) vinegar: rice or apple cider
Sriracha sauce or ground white pepper, to taste
1 tsp sesame seed oil
1½ to 2 cups of vegetables, several kinds, cut up, such as:

mustard greens	cauliflower	bok choy	celery
green beans	asparagus	zucchini	kale
beet greens	snow peas	spinach	corn
mushrooms	eggplant	carrot	peas

1 egg, lightly beaten
2 slices tofu, cubed or sliced
Cilantro as garnish (optional)

- In a baggie, marinate pork slices in soy sauce, 20 minutes.
- In a soup pot, sauté chopped onion in olive oil, 5 minutes.
- Add in chicken stock, marinated pork and its soy sauce, vinegar, Sriracha, and sesame seed oil. Bring to boil. Reduce heat to low. Cook 5 minutes.
- Add in vegetables. Bring to boil. Reduce heat to low. Cook 10 minutes.
- Add in a lightly beaten (raw) egg and stir. Add in tofu. Top with cilantro.

Serves 3.

Note: We vary the vegetables. Sometimes we cook pork **or** chicken (not both). As Steve says, "It's different every time."

Quick Chicken Soup

Well, sometimes we have no leftover Chicken-in-a-Pot. *So, we make* Quick Chicken Soup, *and, just like* Real Chicken Soup, *our troubles melt away as soon as that broth begins to bubble. (Choose a few vegetables from this big list.)*

A carbohydrate ("carb"): rice, egg noodles, or cubed boiled potatoes
1 Tbsp olive oil
1 cup of chicken pieces: either leftover or raw
1/4 cup onion, chopped
2 cups of vegetables, several kinds, cut into bite sizes:

mustard greens	mushrooms	zucchini	carrot
yellow squash	cauliflower	broccoli	corn
green beans	lima beans	spinach	peas
bell pepper	tomatoes	celery	kale

1 to 3 seasonings, to taste: curry, basil, oregano, poultry seasoning
Ground pepper, to taste: black, cayenne, or white
1 can (14 oz) canned chicken broth

➤ Start cooking your "carb." Set it aside when done.
➤ In a soup pot, sauté chicken and onions in olive oil. (If using already-cooked chicken, no need to sauté it; add it in with the vegetables.)
➤ When chicken is done, add in seasonings and vegetables. Cook, covered, on low, 5 minutes.
➤ Add in broth. Bring to a boil. Lower heat and cook, covered, 5 to 10 minutes.
➤ To serve, scoop your "carb" into individual bowls and then ladle in the soup.

Serves 2 to 3.

Note: Chicken and a "carb" are optional—your soup can be broth and vegetables with seasonings. Make it work for *you*.

Tomato Vegetable Stew

1 very small potato (1/2 to 3/4 cup chopped)
2 Tbsps chopped onion
3 Tbsps olive oil (divided)
Oregano, rosemary and/or basil, to taste
Ground pepper, to taste: black, cayenne, and/or white

1½ cups of vegetables, several kinds, in bite sizes, such as:

mushrooms	broccoli	celery
bell pepper	cabbage	corn
cauliflower	carrot	peas

1 can (14.5 oz) stewed tomatoes
1 can (5.5 oz) tomato juice
1 cup beef broth
1 cup canned white beans *or* kidney beans, drained*
1/2 cup cut up squash: yellow, zucchini, leftover acorn *or* butternut
1 cup torn "leaves": beet greens, kale, mustard greens, *or* spinach

- Put potatoes in a dish of water. Microwave about 3 minutes. Set aside.
- In a soup pot, sauté onions in 1 tablespoon olive oil, until golden, about 5 minutes.
- Add in seasonings, potatoes, the 1½ cups of vegetables, and 2 tablespoons olive oil. (If using kale, add it in now.) Cover and cook on medium-low, 5 minutes. Stir occasionally.
- Add in tomato products, beef broth, and beans. Bring to a boil, then reduce heat to low (barely bubbling) and cook, covered, about 7 minutes.
- Add in the squash and "leaves" and cook on low, covered, about 7 minutes.

Serves 4 to 5.

Note: *With the 3/4 cup of leftover beans, you could make a small *River Bean Salad* (see recipe in Salad section).

Shelly's Borscht

Part 1
1 bunch beets:
    3 large beets, cubed and
    stems & leaves, chopped
1½ cups water + 1/4 tsp salt

Part 2
1 can (14 oz) beef broth*
1/4 cup red or white wine
1 cup cubed potato
1 cup chopped onion

Part 3
1 cup sliced carrot
1 cup sliced celery
Basil, to taste
Tarragon, to taste
Black pepper, to taste

Plain yogurt, to top**

- Bring water and salt to a boil in a large saucepan. Add beets and stems. Bring back to a boil. Cook, covered, on medium-low heat, 15 minutes.
- You'll want beets *al dente* or else they'll lose their rich flavor.
    - If beets are *al dente* at 15 minutes, set them and its beet broth aside.
    - If beets aren't done yet, continue to boil. Monitor closely.
- Meanwhile, pour beef broth and wine into a soup pot. Add in potato, onion, and seasonings. Bring to a boil. Reduce heat to low (gentle bubble) and cook, covered, 5 to 10 minutes.
- Spoon/pour the *al dente* beets and its *beet* broth into your soup pot. Add in carrot and celery. Bring to a boil. Reduce heat to low. Cook, covered, about 10 minutes.
- Serve in soup bowls, topping each with plain yogurt.

Serves 4.

Notes:
* Instead of canned broth, you can use stock from *California Pot Roast* or *Steve's Beef Stew* (see recipes in Beef section).
**You can use sour cream (which is traditional) instead of yogurt.

Classic Lentil Soup

3/4 cup dry lentils
2 cups water
1 can (14 oz) chicken broth
      or **2 cups leftover *Chicken-in-a-Pot* stock, with or w/o chicken**
      or **use <u>no</u> broth and add in another 1¾ cups water**
1/2 cup white wine
1/4 cup olive oil
3/4 cup (1 small) chopped onion
1/2 tsp Italian Seasonings
Ground black pepper, to taste
3/4 cup carrot, chopped or sliced
3/4 cup celery, chopped or sliced

- Soak the lentils for 2 to 3 hours.
- Put water, chicken broth, wine, oil, onions, and seasonings in a soup pot. Bring to a boil, then reduce heat to medium-low (gentle boil).
- Drain and rinse the lentils in a colander. Then add lentils to the soup pot.
- Bring soup back to a boil, then lower heat and cook (barely bubbling), mostly covered, about 75 minutes, stirring occasionally.
- Two choices for carrots and celery:
  - steam them separately for about 7 minutes, *or*
  - add them to the soup pot during the last 10 minutes.

Serves 3 or 4.

Notes:
- Add a sliced Italian or German-style sausage if that appeals.
- You can make this soup in a slow cooker. Use 1 cup of water instead of 2. See your manufacturer's instructions for cook time.

Lentil Soup with Sun-Dried Tomatoes

About twenty years ago, Steve looked in the refrigerator for something new to add to his lentil soup. He emerged with sun-dried tomatoes. Sounded odd to me, but it's actually really good, especially when you add in oil from the sun-dried tomato jar.

3/4 cup dry lentils
2 cups water
1 can (14 oz) chicken broth
      ***or* 2 cups leftover *Chicken-in-a-Pot* stock, with or w/o chicken**
      ***or* use <u>no</u> broth and add in another 1¾ cups water**
1/2 cup white wine
2 Tbsps olive oil
3/4 cup (1 small) chopped onion
1/2 tsp Italian Seasonings
Ground black pepper, to taste
2 Tbsps sun-dried tomatoes, chopped
2 Tbsps oil from sun-dried tomato jar
3/4 cup carrot, chopped or sliced
3/4 cup celery, chopped or sliced

- Soak the lentils for 2 to 3 hours.
- Put water, chicken broth, wine, oil, onions, and seasonings in a soup pot. Bring to a boil, then reduce heat to medium-low (gentle boil).
- Drain and rinse the lentils in a colander. Add lentils to the soup pot.
- Bring soup back to a boil, then lower heat and cook (barely bubbling), mostly covered, about 75 minutes, stirring occasionally.
- Add in the sun-dried tomatoes and their oil, during the last 10 minutes.
- Two choices for carrots and celery:
  - steam them separately for about 7 minutes, *or*
  - add them to the soup pot during the last 10 minutes.

Serves 3 or 4.

Lentil Soup with Tomatoes

Steve's Lentil Soup with Sun-Dried Tomatoes *is awesome, but what if you don't have sun-dried tomatoes? One afternoon, on my way home from Tai Chi, I stopped at a grocery store for sun-dried tomatoes, but they didn't carry them. I wanted to make Steve's soup—already had the lentils soaking at home. Not wanting to go to a second store—but wanting tomatoes in my lentil soup!—I bought canned diced tomatoes. To my surprise, this worked just fine! (Whole tomatoes are also good.)*

3/4 cup dry lentils
2 cups water
1 can (14 oz) chicken broth
    or **2 cups leftover** *Chicken-in-a-Pot* **stock, with or w/o chicken**
    or **use no broth and add in another 1¾ cups water**
1 can (14 oz) whole *or* **diced tomatoes**
1/2 cup white wine
1/4 cup olive oil
3/4 cup (1 small) chopped onion
1/2 tsp Italian Seasonings
Ground black pepper, to taste
1/2 cup carrot, chopped (optional)
1/2 cup celery, chopped (optional)

- Soak the lentils for 2 to 3 hours.
- Put water, chicken broth, tomatoes, wine, oil, onions, and seasonings in a soup pot. Bring to a boil, then reduce heat to medium-low (gentle boil).
- Drain and rinse the lentils in a colander. Then add lentils to the soup pot.
- Bring soup back to a boil, then lower heat and cook (barely bubbling), mostly covered, about 75 minutes, stirring occasionally.
- Two choices for (the optional) carrots and celery:
    - steam them separately for about 7 minutes, *or*
    - add them to the soup pot during the last 10 minutes.

Serves 3 or 4.

Irene's Split Pea Soup

It was my friend Eric's mom, Irene, who introduced me to yellow split peas, saying she preferred them over the green. This was in the late 1970s in her San Francisco Victorian. As he was growing up, Eric watched Irene make split pea soup and he, in turn, taught me how to cook it. I never wrote down the recipe; this is my best guess, and I have tested it.

- **1 cup dry split peas: green or yellow—soaked overnight in water**
- **1 ham bone***
- **3 cups water**
- **1 can (14 oz) chicken broth**
  - *or* 2 cups leftover *Chicken-in-a-Pot* stock, with or w/o chicken
- **1/2 cup (or more) white wine**
- **3/4 cup chopped onion**
- **3/4 cup sliced carrots**
- **3/4 cup sliced celery**

➢ Soak the peas **overnight** in a medium bowl of water in the refrigerator.
➢ Bring to a boil 3 cups water, broth, wine, and onion in a soup pot. Lower heat to medium-low (gentle bubble).
➢ Drain and rinse peas in a colander. Then add peas to the soup pot.
➢ Bring soup back to a boil. Reduce heat and cook (gentle bubble) for 2 hours, partly covered, stirring occasionally.
➢ Two choices for carrots and celery: Steam them separately for about 7 minutes, *or* add them in to the soup pot during the last 10 minutes.

Serves 5.

Notes: *Instead of a ham bone, you can add in chunks of ham *or* use no ham at all. If you opt for no ham, add in seasonings, such as basil, salt, and pepper.

Steve's Split Pea Soup

Steve pours beer into the pot instead of white wine.

1 cup dry split peas: green or yellow—soaked overnight in water
1 ham bone*
2 cups water
1 can (14 oz) chicken broth
   or 2 cups leftover *Chicken-in-a-Pot* stock, with or w/o chicken
1 can (12 oz) beer
3/4 cup chopped onion
3/4 cup sliced carrots
3/4 cup sliced celery

- Soak the peas **overnight** in a medium bowl of water in the refrigerator.
- Bring to a boil 3 cups water, broth, beer, and onion in a soup pot. Lower heat to medium-low (gentle bubble).
- Drain and rinse peas in a colander. Then add peas to the soup pot.
- Bring soup back to a boil. Reduce heat and cook (gentle bubble) for 2 hours, partly covered, stirring occasionally.
- Two choices for carrots and celery: Steam them separately for about 7 minutes, *or* add them in to the soup pot during the last 10 minutes.

Serves 5.

Notes: *Instead of a ham bone, you can add in chunks of ham *or* use no ham at all. If you opt for no ham, add in seasonings, such as basil, salt, and pepper.

Noe Valley Corn Chowder

2 small potatoes (1½ cups when cubed)
1/2 cup (or more) chopped onion
2 Tbsps olive oil (divided)
2 cups of vegetables, several kinds, cut into bite sizes, such as:
    green beans   cauliflower   cabbage   celery
    mushrooms   broccoli   carrot   peas
Ground black pepper, to taste
1 can (14 oz) chicken broth
    or 2 cups leftover *Chicken-in-a-Pot* stock, with or w/o chicken
Corn, two options:
    Option A: 1/2 cup corn—fresh, frozen, or canned kernels
        and 1 cup (or more) cream-style corn
    Option B: 9 oz (1 small can) corn
1/2 cup milk (optional)

- Place whole potatoes in bubbling water and boil 25 to 30 minutes. (I leave skins on, but feel free to peel them.) Set aside. Cut into bite sizes.
- Meanwhile, in a soup pot, sauté the onion in 1 tablespoon olive oil, about 5 minutes.
- Add in cubed potato, vegetables (*except* the cream-style corn), 1 tablespoon oil, and black pepper. Cook, covered, on low heat, about 10 minutes.
- Add broth and cream-style corn to the soup pot. Bring to a boil then lower heat (gentle bubble) and cook, covered, 10 to 15 minutes.
- Add in milk. Bring soup back to a gentle bubble, and then *immediately* turn heat off.

Serves 4 or 5.

Note: For extra flavor, add a sliced German-style sausage to the soup pot or a pat of butter in your soup bowl.

Shrimp in Corn Chowder

This recipe is simply Noe Valley Corn Chowder *(see recipe) with shrimp added to your soup bowl.*

Frozen cooked shrimp, deveined—enough for the number of people who will be eating this chowder today*
Noe Valley Corn Chowder (see recipe)

➢ Defrost shrimp according to directions on the package.
➢ Serve the chowder in soup bowls.
➢ Add the shrimp to each individual bowl.*

Serves 4 or 5.

Note: *The idea is to keep the shrimp out of the soup pot. This way, if you have leftover chowder, there will be no shrimp in tomorrow's leftovers. Just wouldn't want you to have any GI problems tomorrow from shrimp that has been in leftover chowder for an extended time.

Veggies in Vegetable Broth

1/4 cup uncooked brown rice
2 cups of boxed vegetable broth
1/4 cup white wine, preferably sweet
1/4 cup diced onion
1/2 to 1 tsp curry powder
1/2 tsp basil
Salt, to taste: garlic, table or seasoned
Ground pepper, to taste: black, cayenne, or white
1½ to 2 cups vegetables, several kinds, in bite sizes, such as:

green beans	eggplant	hominy	corn
cauliflower	broccoli	carrots	peas

- Cook brown rice according to directions on the package.
- Pour the broth and wine into a soup pot. Add onion and seasonings.
- Bring to a boil, then lower heat to low and cook, covered, 5 to 10 minutes.
- Add in the vegetables. Bring back to a boil, then reduce heat to low. Cook, covered, until the veggies are done, 7 to 10 minutes.
- To serve, scoop rice in individual bowls, then ladle in soup.

Serves 2 to 3.

Note: The recipes *Magic Minestrone, Tomato Vegetable Stew,* and *Veggies in Vegetable Broth* are similar, yet each one is unique.

Stovetop Pot of Beans

1 cup dry beans: kidney and/or pinto
2 quarts cold water
Chicken broth: 1 can (14 oz) chicken broth
      or **2 cups leftover** *Chicken-in-a-Pot* **stock**
1 tsp chili powder
1/2 tsp cumin
1/2 tsp salt
1/8 tsp ground cayenne pepper
1½ cups chopped onion (Red onion is good.)
1 cup chopped celery
Grated cheese, as topping (optional)

- Soak the beans in a bowl of water overnight in the refrigerator.
- The next day put 2 quarts of water, along with broth and seasonings, in a large pot. Bring to a boil.
- Meanwhile, drain and rinse the beans.
- Add the beans, onion, and celery to the pot.
- Reduce heat to medium-low (gentle boil) and cook, partially covered, until beans are tender, about 3 ½ hours.
- Check every so often and stir.
- Top each bowl with grated cheese.

Serves 4 or 5.

Note: You can also add in salsa to the soup pot.

How Much Seasonings to Use?

I'm not comfy writing in the exact amount of seasonings to use. Here's why:

- People's *palates* and *preferences* differ. What is too much for one person is not enough for another.

- Spices and herbs lose their *potency* over time. Every so often, I toss a bottle of seasoning and replace it with a fresh one because it no longer has any flavor.

- There is variation of taste and strength among *crops*, and so two bottles of dried seasonings may taste different from each other.

- *Fresh* herbs and spices taste different from *dried* ones. Years ago I used fresh sage that a friend had picked in Nevada. Not knowing it was extremely potent, I unwittingly used way too much and absolutely ruined a chicken dish. Steve and I have written these recipes for *dried* spices, although we personally grow our own basil and rosemary.

Ham and Bean Soup
(in a Slow Cooker)

Give the beans an overnight soak in the refrigerator. Next day, throw it all in the slow cooker and let the electric pot work its magic!

1 ham hock
1 cup dry beans: red, white, black or pinto
1½ cups water
1¾ cups (one 14 oz can) chicken broth
1 cup chopped onion
1½ cups sliced carrot
1½ cups sliced celery
Sage, to taste
Italian Seasonings, to taste
Ground pepper, to taste: black, cayenne or white
Grated cheese, as a topping (optional)

- Soak the beans in a bowl of water in the refrigerator *overnight*.
- The next day rinse the beans.
- Place all ingredients, *except* cheese, in a slow cooker and cook until beans are tender. Slow cookers vary in cook time so we can't say exactly how long you should cook your soup. See your manufacturer's recommendations. Also, different kinds of beans vary in cook time.
- Top each bowl with grated cheese.

Serves 6.

Note: You can also add salsa to the soup pot.

Vegetarian Bean Soup
(in a Slow Cooker)

This recipe is basically Ham and Bean Soup *without the ham.*

3/4 cup dry beans: red, white, black, or pinto
1/2 to 1 cup water
1¾ cups (one 14 oz can) chicken broth
1 cup chopped onion
1 cup sliced carrot
1 cup sliced celery
Sage, to taste
Italian Seasonings, to taste
Ground pepper, to taste: black, cayenne or white
Grated cheese, as a topping (optional)

➢ Soak the beans in a bowl of water in the refrigerator overnight.
➢ The next day rinse the beans.
➢ Place all ingredients, *except* cheese, in a slow cooker and cook until beans are tender. Slow cookers vary in cook time so we can't say exactly how long you should cook your soup. It will be several hours. See your manufacturer's recommendations. Also, different kinds of beans vary in cook time.
➢ Top each bowl with grated cheese.

Serves 4 to 5.

Note: You can also add salsa to the soup pot.

Potato Leek Soup in Amsterdam

When Steve lived in Amsterdam in the 1990s, he noticed Dutch grocery stores offered packaged leeks, already washed and cut up. That sort of convenience appealed to him, and he thought about what he wanted to cook with leeks. He decided on leek soup.

Okay, but what should go into this soup besides leeks? Potatoes, he decided. Northern Europeans are big on potatoes; leeks and potatoes would go well together, similar to putting onions in potato soup.

Good, but what for the broth? Beer, he decided, because historically speaking, beer was an everyday beverage. (My Dutch ancestors knew that water straight out of the canal could cause sickness or death. Beer was a solution to this problem, a workaround beverage.)

Steve went to work in his tiny Amsterdam kitchen in his rented apartment and now shares his leek soup recipe on the following page. (His apartment, by the way, was very near Anne Frank's family's home, the one they lived in *before* they went into hiding during World War II. I think that is a fascinating bit of trivia.)

Amsterdam Potato Leek Soup with Beer

One bunch of leeks
3 cups water
3 small potatoes (about 3 cups, cubed)
16 oz beer
1¾ cups (one 14 oz can) chicken broth
2 Tbsps olive oil
1½ tsps thyme or Italian Seasonings
Salt, to taste
1 cup milk
Shredded cheese, to top: sharp cheddar, parmesan, etc.
Optional garnishes: turmeric, paprika, or parsley

- Cut the green part of the leeks off and discard.
- Cut the white part of the leeks in 1/2 inch to 1 inch thick slices. Soak them in a bowl of water to get the dirt out.
- Pour 3 cups of water into a soup pot and turn heat to high.
- Meanwhile, wash potatoes and cut them into cubes. Okay to leave skins on.
- To the soup pot, add all ingredients, *except* milk, cheese, and the garnish. Cover and bring to a boil, then lower heat to medium-low.
- Cook for at least 75 minutes, or until potatoes and leeks are soft.
- A few minutes before serving the soup, pour in the milk. As soon as the broth bubbles, turn the heat off.
- Top with cheese, turmeric (or paprika) and/or parsley.

Serves 6 to 8.

Notes:
- Easy to halve this recipe if you want less soup.
- You can add sliced bratwurst sausage during the last half hour of cooking.

Vegan Potato Leek Soup with Beer

This recipe is the same as Amsterdam Potato Leek Soup with Beer *except that it omits milk and cheese.*

> **One bunch of leeks**
> **3 cups water**
> **3 small potatoes (about 3 cups, cubed)**
> **16 oz beer**
> **2 Tbsps olive oil**
> **1½ tsps thyme or Italian Seasonings**
> **Salt, to taste**
> **Optional garnishes: turmeric, paprika, or parsley**

- Cut the green part of the leeks off and discard.
- Cut the white part of the leeks in 1/2 inch to 1 inch thick slices. Soak them in a bowl of water to get the dirt out.
- Pour 3 cups of water into a soup pot and turn heat to high.
- Meanwhile, wash potatoes and cut them into cubes. Okay to leave skins on.
- To the soup pot, add all ingredients, *except* the garnish. Cover and bring to a boil, then lower heat to medium-low.
- Cook for at least 75 minutes, or until potatoes and leeks are soft.
- Top with turmeric (or paprika) and parsley.

Serves 6 to 8.

Note: Easy to halve this recipe if you want less soup.

Susanne's Ravioli Soup

My friend Susanne told me the ingredients of this recipe and I worked out the amounts. It uses ingredients from both the north of Europe and the south: kale and ravioli.

> **1 Italian or German-style sausage (optional)**
> **1 clove of garlic, minced**
> **1 Tbsp + 2 Tbsps olive oil**
> **1/4 cup chopped onion**
> **4 cups kale, torn in pieces with no stems**
> **1/4 cup + 1/2 cup water**
> **1 teaspoon caraway seeds**
> **1 can (14 oz) chicken broth**
> **8 ravioli, any kind as long as it contains cheese**

- Boil the sausage in a saucepan. Set aside when done.
- In a soup pot, sauté garlic and onion in 1 tablespoon olive oil.
- Add in the kale, 2 tablespoons olive oil, 1/4 cup water, and caraway seeds. Cover and cook on medium-low for about 25 minutes, tossing the kale occasionally.
- Pour in chicken broth, 1/2 cup water, and ravioli. Bring to a boil, then lower heat. Cook, covered, on low (barely bubbling) until ravioli is done. Refer to directions on ravioli package for cook time.
- Slice sausage and put in individual soup bowls and then ladle in soup.

Serves 2.

Note: Susanne says that some of the caraway seeds will sink to the bottom and that it's okay to not eat all of them, just let them sit at the bottom.

Big Timber Hamburger Soup

1/2 lb cooked *Seasoned Beef* (see recipe)*
Beef broth: One 14 oz can beef broth
    or 2 cups leftover pot likker (see *California Pot Roast* recipe)
Tomatoes: One 14 oz can stewed tomatoes
    *or o*ne 14 oz can whole or diced tomatoes
    or 1 cup salsa
1/4 cup red wine
1/2 tsp Worcestershire Sauce
2 Tbsps marinated pimiento, chopped
Half of a 14 oz can of beans, any kind
Pepper, to taste: black, cayenne, white
2 cups of vegetables, several kinds, cut into bite sizes, such as:

yellow squash	mushrooms	parsnip	turnip
green beans	lima beans	spinach	celery
bell pepper	tomatoes	hominy	corn
cauliflower	zucchini	carrot	peas

- Put all ingredients into a soup pot *except the 2 cups of vegetables*.
- Bring to a boil, then lower heat and cook, partially covered, for 10 minutes.
- Add in the vegetables, crunchy ones first, soft ones last.
- Bring back to a boil, then reduce heat and cook on low, partially covered, about 10 minutes, until the veggies are done.

Serves 4.

Note: *A shortcut on cooking the meat: pour a little olive oil into a soup pot, add 1/2 lb ground beef, and cook it without minced garlic or chopped onion.

Capture the Liquid
(when using high-fat ground beef)

If Steve uses high-fat ground beef for Big Timber Hamburger Soup, *he removes the fat using a process he calls "capture the liquid." He says this process gives rich beef flavor without the fat. Here is how he does it.*

High-fat cooked ground beef
Colander
Medium-size bowl

➢ Using a colander, drain the cooked ground beef, capturing the liquid in a bowl underneath.
➢ Spoon the beef that's in the colander back into the soup pot.
➢ Take the bowl with the "captured liquid" and place it in your freezer until the fat coagulates, about 30 minutes.
➢ Remove the bowl from the freezer. Skim the fat off the top and discard it.
➢ What remains in the bowl is beef stock. Spoon it into the soup pot.

Salads

Carrot Broccoli Salad

Broccoli salad reminds me of Lake Tahoe in the summer of 2013. I spent several days at the shores of these turquoise waters, doing nothing. Simply relaxed on the beach with my mom and my sister June. Relaxing—what a concept! Each morning, on our way to the beach, we stopped at a local supermarket and bought sandwiches, potato salad, and broccoli salad, which we stashed in the cooler and brought out at lunchtime. Good times! Steve and I developed this recipe together. More good times!

1½ cups raw broccoli florets, cut in bite sizes
2/3 cup carrot, shredded
1/4 cup mayonnaise
1 tsp sugar
1/2 tsp ground coriander
3 Tbsps raisins*
2 Tbsps sunflower seeds or slivered almonds

- Prepare broccoli and carrot. Set aside.
- In a large mixing bowl, blend mayonnaise, sugar, and coriander.
- Add broccoli and carrot to the mayo mixture. Stir.
- Chill the salad in your refrigerator.
- Just before serving, mix in the raisins and seeds/nuts.

Serves 4.

Note: *Instead of raisins, you can use halved grapes. Or use 1/3 cup chopped orange segments—fresh or canned. Or use a combo of raisins, grapes, and oranges.

Steve's Favorite Potato Salad

2 small potatoes *or* 1 large one (2 cups when cooked and cubed)
1 hard-boiled egg, mashed
2 Tbsps mayonnaise
2 Tbsps mustard
Salt, to taste: garlic, table salt or seasoned
Ground pepper, to taste: black, cayenne or white
1/4 cup celery, diced
2 Tbsps fresh parsley, minced
1 Tbsp minced onion
6 Manzanilla olives, stuffed with pimientos, sliced
4 maple bourbon pickle slices, minced
1 Tbsp pickle juice

- Wash potatoes. (We leave skins on but feel free to peel them.)
- Place potatoes in boiling water and cook for 25 to 35 minutes. (Cook time depends on the size of the potatoes.)
- Meanwhile, mix all ingredients, *except* potatoes, in a large bowl.
- When potatoes are done, cut them into bite sizes. Lightly salt them. Let cool.
- Add potato chunks to the mayo mixture. Stir.

Serves 3 or 4.

Various Versions of Potato Salad

With this recipe, you use a basic set of ingredients and then add in more. It all depends on what you have in your kitchen and the taste you want today.

The basic ingredients:
2 small potatoes *or* 1 large one (2 cups when cooked and cubed)
1 hard-boiled egg, mashed
1 to 2 Tbsps mayonnaise
1 to 2 Tbsps mustard
Salt, to taste: garlic, table salt or seasoned
Ground pepper, to taste: black, cayenne or white

Add one or more of these ingredients:
1/4 cup celery, diced
2 Tbsps (or more) fresh parsley, minced
2 Tbsps carrot, shredded
1 to 2 Tbsps pickles, diced *or* pickle relish *or* 5 slices, diced
1 to 2 Tbsps onion, minced
1 Tbsp capers
6 olives, sliced, any kind
6 marinated artichoke hearts, trimmed and chopped
1 Tbsp pickle juice
Dried dill, to taste
1 Tbsp marinated pimiento *or* red bell pepper

- Wash potatoes. (We leave skins on but feel free to peel them.)
- Place potatoes in boiling water and cook for 25 to 35 minutes.
- Meanwhile, mix all ingredients, *except* potatoes, in a large bowl.
- When potatoes are done, salt them, let cool, and cut into bite sizes.
- When they are cool, add the potato bites to the mixture. Stir.

Serves 3 to 4.

Curry Potato Salad

I remember the first time I used curry powder in a potato salad. It was in our Montana kitchen, and I didn't tell Steve. I wanted a new taste in the potato salad, so I shook in a little bit of the yellow powder and served the salad at our next meal. Steve liked it and so did I. Since then I've become bolder—measuring in more and more as time goes by.

2 small potatoes *or* 1 large one (2 cups when cooked and cubed)
1/4 cup diced celery
2 Tbsps diced onion
2 Tbsps pickle relish
1 Tbsp mayonnaise
1 tsp (or more) curry powder
1 tsp (or more) prepared mustard
Salt, to taste: garlic, table salt or seasoned
Ground pepper, to taste: black, cayenne or white

- Wash potatoes. (We leave skins on but feel free to peel them.)
- Place potatoes in boiling water and cook for 25 to 35 minutes. (Cook time depends on the size of the potatoes and how soft you like them.)
- Meanwhile, mix all ingredients, *except* potatoes, in a large bowl.
- When potatoes are done, cut them into bite sizes. Lightly salt them. Let cool.
- Add potato chunks to the mayo mixture. Stir.

Serves 3.

O & V Bleu Cheese Crumbles Potato Salad

1 large potato or 2 small ones (2 cups when cubed)
1/4 cup diced celery
1 Tbsp capers
6 artichoke hearts, chopped and trimmed
1 Tbsp "juice" from the artichoke heart jar
1 Tbsp vinegar (apple, rice, white or wine)
1 Tbsp olive oil
Garlic salt or table salt, to taste
Ground black pepper, to taste
Bleu cheese crumbles or gorgonzola, to taste

- Wash potatoes. (We leave skins on but feel free to peel them.)
- Place potatoes in boiling water and cook for 25 to 35 minutes. (Cook time depends on the size of the potatoes and how soft you like them.)*
- Meanwhile, mix all ingredients, except potatoes, in a large bowl.
- When potatoes are done, cut into bite sizes *or* mash into lumpy mashed potatoes.
- Add potato chunks to the large bowl. Stir.
- Serve and top with bleu cheese crumbles.

Serves 3.

Note: *People differ in their texture preference for potatoes. Some folks like them *al dente*. Others like them almost mashed. Still others like them in between *al dente* and mashed—soft, just at the point where the potato wants to mash.

J&S Macaroni Salad

*Steve and I have taken my mom's macaroni salad recipe and added more stuff. We use the basic ingredients and then **choose** from the list of other ingredients.*

The basic ingredients:
1 cup uncooked Ditalini
1/4 tsp salt
1 tsp vegetable oil (for the cooked pasta)
2 to 3 Tbsps mayonnaise
1/2 cup sharp cheese, cubed or shredded
1/4 cup diced celery
2 Tbsps marinated pimiento, diced
Basil, to taste
Salt, to taste
Cayenne pepper, to taste
Paprika or turmeric, to top

Add one or more of these ingredients:
6 marinated artichoke hearts, trimmed and chopped
8 black ripe olives, chopped
1 Tbsp onion, diced
2 Tbsps capers
2 Tbsps fresh parsley, diced

- Cook pasta according to directions on package. Add 1/4 tsp salt.
- Drain pasta in a colander. Drizzle 1/2 tsp of oil over the pasta. Stir.
- Cool pasta (still in the colander) in the refrigerator.
- Transfer the cooled pasta to a bowl and mix in mayonnaise.
- Add in all of the other ingredients (except paprika) and stir.
- Sprinkle paprika across the top of the salad.

Serves 5 or 6.

Mediterranean Pasta Salad

When I think of pasta salad, I "see" olive-green colored hills and sleepy sun-drenched houses that look out over an azure Mediterranean Sea. Those little white dots out on the water are boats—fishing boats.

> 3/4 cup uncooked Ditalini (or Rotini or Bowtie)
> 1/8 tsp salt
> 1 Tbsp onion, diced or thin slices
> 12 thin slices of cucumber *or* 1/4 cup diced celery
> 1/4 tsp Italian Seasonings
> 1 Tbsp olive oil
> 1 Tbsp vinegar
> 1 Tbsp "juice" from the marinated artichoke jar
> 8 marinated artichoke hearts, trimmed and chopped
> 12 olives, any kind
> 1/4 cup crumbled feta cheese
>
> **Optional:**
> > 1/4 cup fresh parsley, diced
> > 2 Tbsps diced marinated pimento *or* diced red bell pepper
> > 1 small chopped tomato *or* a few cherry tomatoes

- Cook pasta according to directions on package. Throw 1/8 tsp salt in the pot. When pasta is done, drain in a colander and stir in a little oil. Cool pasta (still in the colander) in refrigerator.
- In a large mixing bowl, soak onion, cucumber (or celery), and seasonings in a tablespoon each of olive oil, vinegar, and artichoke jar "juice."
- When pasta is cool, add it to the mixing bowl. Stir.
- Add in everything else: artichoke hearts, olives, feta, and the "optionals." Stir.
- Taste and decide if you want more oil, vinegar, artichoke "juice" and/or seasonings.

Serves 4.

Sherry's Spaghetti Salad

My Tai Chi friend, Sherry, told me about this dish. It can be made from last night's spaghetti, although the recipe below is from scratch. No quantities given, as it depends on your own particular taste preferences.

Spaghetti *or* **other pasta**
Olive oil
Italian red sauce: from a jar *or*
        Joey's Marinara (see recipe in This and That section)
One or all of the following vegetables, chopped up:
    Tomatoes
    Cucumber
    Bell pepper
    Olives, any kind
    Sun-dried tomatoes
    Artichoke hearts, trimmed

- Cook the pasta according to instructions on the package.
- When the pasta is done, drain it in a colander. Mix in a little oil so that the pasta doesn't stick together.
- Transfer pasta to a mixing bowl and mix in the red sauce. Cool in your refrigerator.
- Cut up the vegetables.
- Add vegetables to the pasta and red sauce. Stir.

> Note: This dish can sit in the refrigerator overnight and be eaten the next day.

Shrimp Parmesan Orzo Salad

The key to this salad, Steve says, is parmesan. He coached me through the basics when we lived in Montana, and since then we've used various ingredients. Choose one dressing and a few vegetables from the list.

> 4 to 6 oz frozen shrimp (8 to 12 large size) cooked and deveined
> 1/2 cup uncooked Orzo
> 1/8 tsp salt and 1/2 tsp canola oil
> 1 Tbsp teriyaki sauce (or soy sauce)
> Dressing, such as:
>> *Tahini Salad Dressing* (see recipe) *or*
>> *Citrus Sesame Oil Salad Dressing* (see recipe) *or*
>> **Bottled Goddess dressing** *or*
>> **Balsamic vinegar, olive oil, dash of Italian Seasonings** *or*
>> **Juice from the artichoke jar**
>
> 3 or more vegetables, cut up, such as:
>> 2 Tbsps marinated pimiento
>> 6 marinated artichoke hearts
>> 1/4 cup peas   8 olives
>> 1/4 cup celery   1 Tbsp onion
>> 1/4 cup broccoli   2 Tbsps capers
>> 1/4 cup corn kernels
>
> 1/3 cup shredded parmesan cheese

- Thaw shrimp according to directions on the package.
- Cook orzo according to directions on package. Add salt. When done, drain orzo in a colander. Stir in 1/2 tsp oil. Cool (still in the colander) in the refrigerator.
- Place shrimp in a small bowl. Mix in teriyaki sauce. Refrigerate.
- Make your dressing.
- Combine in a large bowl: cooled orzo, dressing, vegetables, and cheese. Stir.
- Serve in individual bowls and add shrimp to each of them.

Serves 3 or 4.

Chicken Parmesan Orzo Salad

Similar to the recipe for Shrimp Parmesan Orzo Salad. *Fewer steps. Choose one dressing and a few vegetables from the list.*

1 cup already cooked chicken, chopped*
1/2 cup uncooked Orzo
1/8 tsp salt
1/2 tsp canola oil
Dressing, such as:
    Tahini Salad Dressing **(see recipe)** *or*
    Citrus Sesame Oil Salad Dressing **(see recipe)** *or*
    Bottled Goddess dressing *or*
    Balsamic vinegar, olive oil, dash of Italian Seasonings *or*
    Juice from the artichoke jar

3 or more vegetables, cut up, such as:
    2 Tbsps marinated pimiento
    6 marinated artichoke hearts
    1/4 cup peas   **8 olives**
    1/4 cup celery   **1 Tbsp onion**
    1/4 cup broccoli   **2 Tbsps capers**
    1/4 cup corn kernels

1/3 cup shredded parmesan cheese

- Cook orzo according to directions on package. Add salt. When done, drain orzo in a colander. Stir in 1/2 tsp oil. Cool orzo (still in the colander) in the refrigerator.
- Make your dressing.
- In a large bowl, combine cooled orzo, dressing, chicken, vegetables, and cheese. Stir.

Serves 3 or 4.

Note: *You can use leftover chicken from *Chicken-in-a-Pot*.

Tahini Salad Dressing

It was Michelle in Isla Vista who introduced me to tahini one laidback summer evening during my student days at UC Santa Barbara. She served a green salad with a tahini-based dressing, and I remember thinking, Wow, I've never tasted anything like this before! I asked her what tahini was, and she said it was made from sesame seeds. Michelle, wherever you are, I hope you are still enjoying the exotic flavor of tahini.

Here is a flavorful tahini salad dressing recipe Steve came up with.

> **1/2 clove garlic, minced***
> **2 Tbsps lime juice *or* lemon juice *or* white wine**
> **1 Tbsp olive oil**
> **1 Tbsp honey**
> **3 Tbsps tahini paste**
> **Ground white pepper, to taste**
> **Salt, to taste**
> **A few tsps cold water (optional)**

- Sauté the minced garlic in olive oil.*
- In a bowl, combine garlic with citrus juice (or wine), oil, honey, tahini paste, white pepper, and salt. Stir until blended.
- Add in cold water, one teaspoonful at a time, and stir, until you have the desired consistency. (Optional)
- Chill and marinate in the refrigerator.
- Pour dressing onto your salad.

Serves 2.

Note: *Instead of fresh garlic, you could use garlic powder or garlic salt. Or omit garlic entirely.

Citrus Sesame Oil Salad Dressing

1 Tbsp lemon juice *or* lime juice
1 Tbsp olive oil
1 tsp honey
1 tsp sesame oil
Ground ginger, to taste
Ground white pepper, to taste

Two ways to make this. One way:
- Whisk ingredients in a small bowl. When you're ready to put it on your salad, stir the dressing vigorously and immediately pour.

Or make it like this:
- Whisk ingredients in a large salad bowl. Then add your salad ingredients to the large bowl and mix.

Serves 2.

Note: Taste and see if it's right for *you* because this is really an individual thing.
- Not tart enough? Add more citrus.
- Too tart? Add more honey and/or a little bit of water.
- Want a richer flavor? Add more oil.
- Too intense? Add a little bit of water or oil.
- Want it zingier? Add more ginger.
- Want it hotter? Add more pepper.

Deluxe Salad

If you use even one-third of these ingredients, you will have a deluxe salad. It can be different every time, depending on the ingredients you have on hand and your preferences in the moment. The amounts are up to you.

    Lettuces (any kind you like)
    Seafood: canned tuna, cold cooked prawns, or cold cooked ahi
    Ham, chopped
    Cooked chicken, chopped*
    Hard-boiled egg, chopped
    Fruit: Bartlett pear, strawberries, orange, apple, raspberries, etc.
    Avocado: halved, sliced, chopped, or guacamole
    Cold cooked peas
    Cold cooked asparagus
    Shredded carrot
    Sliced celery
    Chopped mushrooms
    Chopped cabbage
    Chopped broccoli
    Pickled beets
    Canned beans: chick peas, green beans, kidneys, etc.
    Cheese: feta, bleu, shredded parmesan, etc.
    Nuts: pecans, walnuts, almonds, etc.
    Seeds: sunflower, pumpkin, sesame, etc.

- Build your salad.
- Drizzle salad dressing over your salad (see various salad recipes).

Note: *You can use leftover chicken from *Chicken-in-a-Pot*.

Maple Mustard Salad Dressing

1 Tbsp balsamic vinegar
1 Tbsp olive oil
1/2 tsp mustard (Dijon is good.)
1/2 tsp pure maple syrup
Ground white pepper, to taste

Two ways to make this. One way:
- Whisk ingredients in a small bowl. When you're ready to put it on your salad, stir the dressing vigorously and immediately pour.

Or make it like this:
- Whisk ingredients in a large salad bowl. Then add your salad ingredients to the large bowl.

Serves 2.

Three Sisters Salad

**1 cup chopped lettuce (any kind)
1/2 cup chopped cold cooked cauliflower
1/2 cup chopped tomatoes**

- Make *Maple Mustard Salad Dressing* (see recipe) in a mixing bowl.
- Add in the vegetables and toss.

Serves 2.

Three Sisters and a Brother Salad

**1 or more kinds of torn or chopped lettuce, enough for 2 people
1/2 chopped avocado
1/3 cup cold cooked sliced carrots
1/3 cup cold cooked peas
1/3 cup chopped tomatoes (optional)**

- Make *Maple Mustard Salad Dressing* (see recipe) in a mixing bowl.
- Add in the vegetables and toss.

Serves 2.

St. Patrick's Day Salad Dressing and Salad

When you puree yogurt and parsley, you get a green-colored salad dressing. Tastes great any day, but is especially fun on St. Patrick's Day. I've included a salad recipe to go along with the dressing.

Dressing:	**Salad:**
1/2 cup plain Greek yogurt	Lettuce, chopped
1/2 cup fresh parsley, minced	Tomato, chopped
1 Tbsp milk or water (opt.)	Avocado bites
Salt, to taste	Olives, any kind
Ground pepper, to taste	Feta cheese (optional)

Making the Dressing:
- Wash and partially dry parsley.
- Put the yogurt and parsley in a blender. Blend until the parsley is pureed.
- If the mixture is too thick, add milk (or water).
- Add in salt and pepper, to taste.

Making the Salad:
- Put chopped lettuce in a large bowl. Pour in the dressing from the blender.*
- Mix thoroughly.
- Add in tomatoes, avocado, and olives. Mix with care.
- Serve in individual bowls. Top with feta cheese.

Serves 2 or 3.

Note: *If you have dressing left over, I would recommend that you NOT keep it.

Jannie's Creamy Yogurt Salad Dressing

This is an adaptation of my St Patrick's Day Salad Dressing *(see recipe). Main differences are that this recipe uses a lot of dried dill, a little bit of parsley, and no blender.*

> **1/4 cup plain yogurt**
> **3/4 tsp dried dill**
> **Basil, to taste**
> **Salt, to taste: garlic, table or seasoned**
> **Ground black pepper, to taste**
> **Ground cayenne pepper, to taste**
> **1 or 2 Tbsps minced fresh parsley (optional)**

Two ways to make this. One way:
➢ Mix ingredients in a small bowl with a spoon.

Or make it like this:
➢ Mix ingredients in a large salad bowl with a spoon. Then add your salad ingredients to the large bowl.

Serves 2.

Note: *If you have dressing left over, I would recommend that you NOT keep it.

Chris's California Salad

The amounts are up to you.

Cucumber, peeled and thinly sliced
Olive oil
Red wine vinegar or balsamic vinegar
Lettuce, 2 or more kinds: red leaf, green leaf, Romaine, butter
Tomato, slices
Olives, any kind
Avocado, chopped
Ground black pepper, to taste
Artichoke hearts, trimmed and chopped

- On a plate, soak cucumber slices in olive oil and vinegar.
- In a large bowl, mix together the lettuces, tomato, avocado, olives, and artichoke hearts.
- Mix in the now-marinated cucumber, along with the marinade. Shake in black pepper.
- Taste the salad and decide if you need to add more oil and/or vinegar.
- Transfer all of this to a serving bowl.

Note: This is one of those fun salads where you dig in with an oversized spoon and fork and find delectable vegetables hiding among the oil-and-vinegar-coated lettuce.

Loretta's Salad

I had this supervisor once—I'll call her Loretta—and she and I would sometimes "do" salad bar at lunchtime. The combination of ingredients Loretta chose were different from mine up until then, but after suffering from Salad Envy several times, I started imitating her, and have done so many times since. Here are the ingredients Loretta chose to make her delicious salad.

Lettuce
Baby spinach
Hard-boiled egg, chopped
Kidney beans
Cold peas
Beets

Note: Loretta chose *Thousand Island* (see recipe) or bleu cheese for her salad dressing.

Thousand Island Salad Dressing

My mom showed me how to make this dressing when I was about 10 years old, and for years afterwards it was my favorite dressing. I was fascinated that I started with three very different ingredients and created something so unlike any one of them. I remember being amazed that it tasted, in my opinion, pretty professional. The only thing I've added to my childhood dressing is hot sauce.

> **1 Tbsp mayonnaise**
> **1 Tbsp ketchup**
> **1 Tbsp pickle relish**
> **Hot sauce, to taste (optional)**

Two ways to make this. One way:
- Mix ingredients in a small bowl with a spoon.

Or make it like this:
- Mix ingredients in a large salad bowl with a spoon. Then add your salad ingredients to the large bowl.

Serves 2.

Steve's Coleslaw

Steve watched his mom make coleslaw when he was a boy and this is basically her recipe. Steve adds in coriander and white pepper.

1 cup grated cabbage, green or purple, packed
1/3 cup shredded carrot*
3 Tbsps mayonnaise
1 Tbsp apple cider vinegar
1/2 tsp sugar (optional)
1/2 tsp coriander
1/4 tsp dill (optional)
Dash of basil
Dash of garlic salt
Dash of white pepper

- Shred cabbage and carrot. Set aside.
- In a medium size bowl, mix all ingredients *except* the cabbage and carrot.
- Now add in the cabbage and carrot. Mix thoroughly.

Serves 2.

Note: *You can omit the carrot and just shred a total of 1 and 1/3 cups cabbage.

In-a-Hurry-No-Refrigerator-Needed Coleslaw

Excerpt from my Cooking in Montana *cookbook, November 2014:*
"The other morning, before work, when I was still half asleep, I made a quick coleslaw. I packed it in two small containers, and Steve and I put them in our respective lunch boxes. At noon, in the lunch room, I peeked into my bag and spied an unfamiliar container. 'What's this?' I wondered. 'Oh, yeah, I made coleslaw this morning when I was half asleep…Hey, coleslaw! Hooray for me!' It was like a gift."

1 Tbsp + 1 tsp apple cider vinegar
2 tsps honey
1 tsp olive oil
1 cup shredded cabbage, packed
Sunflower seeds or slivered almonds, to taste (optional)

➢ Mix the vinegar, honey, and oil together in a bowl.
➢ Add in the cabbage and seeds/nuts. Mix well.

Serves 2.

Note: Don't forget to pack a fork. ☺ Now go seize the day!

Coleslaw with Salsa

Here's an easy recipe. I was served something similar at a fish taco stand in Baja, Mexico during the 1990s. Years later, in Montana, when I wanted to make coleslaw, I put these two ingredients together and, well, I think it tastes muy bien!

1 cup shredded cabbage, packed
Salsa, to taste*

➢ Mix the two ingredients together in a bowl.

Serves 2.

Note: *The amount of salsa totally depends on how hot your salsa is, how hot you like your food, and how tomato-ee you want your coleslaw to be. Could be one tablespoon of salsa, could be 1/4 cup.

River Bean Salad

I used to pack this salad in our lunch bag when Steve and I went rock collecting on the gravel beds of Montana's Yellowstone River. Such beautiful memories.

- **1 can (14 oz) beans, such as: black, kidney, *or* white beans**
- **1/3 cup celery *or* cucumber, chopped**
- **6 marinated artichoke hearts, trimmed and chopped**
- **2 Tbsps "juice" from artichoke jar**
- **2 Tbsps marinated pimiento *or* red bell pepper,* chopped**
- **1 Tbsp onion, minced***
- **2 Tbsps olive oil**
- **2 Tbsps vinegar (any kind)**
- **Dried dill, to taste**
- **One or more herbs, to taste, such as: basil, marjoram, oregano, savory**
- **Ground pepper, to taste: black pepper, cayenne, or white**
- **Feta cheese, to top (optional)**

➢ Drain the beans.
➢ Combine all ingredients *except the beans* and stir until well blended.
➢ Now add in the beans. Stir.
➢ Place in the refrigerator to chill and marinate. Stir every so often.
➢ Top with feta (optional).

Serves 4.

Notes:
*Sometimes I sauté red bell pepper in olive oil to soften it up and bring out its flavor. Other times I like the crunchiness of raw red bell pepper. Same with onion.

**You could make *Citrus Sesame Oil Salad Dressing* (see recipe) instead of using artichoke jar "juice," oil, vinegar, and herbs.

Bean and Corn Salad

Great things can, and do, come from leftovers—this recipe was made from them. I often look in the refrigerator and find ingredients lurking, waiting to become a delicious new dish. This recipe is very similar to River Bean Salad *(see recipe).*

    3/4 cup canned kidney beans
    1/2 cup canned green beans
    1/4 cup canned corn
    1/2 cup diced cucumber
    4 marinated artichoke hearts, trimmed and chopped
    2 Tbsps "juice" from artichoke jar
    1 Tbsp olive oil
    1 Tbsp balsamic vinegar
    Dill, to taste
    Salt, to taste
    Black pepper, to taste

- Drain the beans and corn, separately, in a colander.
- Combine all ingredients *except the beans and corn.* Stir until well blended.
- Now add in the beans and corn. Stir.
- Place in the refrigerator to chill and marinate. Stir every so often.

Serves 3.

Poultry

Turkey Spaghetti

Every so often don't you get a hankering for good ol' spaghetti in meat sauce? You can use ground turkey and get the same satisfaction as beef.

1 lb ground turkey
1 cup chopped onion
1/2 tsp oregano
Ground black pepper, to taste
2 Tbsps chopped marinated sun-dried tomatoes
2 Tbsps oil from sun-dried tomato jar *or* olive oil
1 cup chopped mushrooms
1 cup shredded carrot
One cup of chopped vegetables, at least one kind, such as:
    cauliflower   eggplant   yellow squash
    celery   kale   zucchini
1 can (14 oz) beef broth
1 can (14 oz) crushed tomatoes (Or 28 oz can for more tomato flavor)
2 Tbsps cornstarch and 2 Tbsps water
Pasta, such as spaghetti or angel hair

- In a large skillet, sauté ground turkey, onion, and seasonings. Cook well.
- Add in sun-dried tomato and its oil, plus vegetables. Simmer 5 minutes.
- Add beef broth and crushed tomatoes. Bring to boil. Simmer 5 to 10 minutes.
- Meanwhile, cook pasta according to the directions on the package.
- Thicken sauce: In a cup, mix 2 tablespoons each of cornstarch and cold water. Spoon into the bubbling sauce. May not need all of it.
- Serve over pasta.

Serves 4.

Note: *Vegetables in Mild Marinara Sauce*, in This and That section, is a vegetarian version of this recipe.

An Easier Tomorrow—Having Inventory

I'll get right to the point: *buy food in bulk, divvy it up, and store it in your freezer and refrigerator.*

When Steve buys meat and poultry, he has the future in mind: he buys large-size packages, divides them up, and freezes them. Some of the meat/poultry is left in larger pieces and part of it is cut into bite sizes or thin strips. He stores all of it in freezer baggies, each one containing the amount we will use for one meal, usually one to two cups of meat, which is dinner for two.

This makes cooking dinner so much easier! With this inventory, we simply pull out a baggie from the freezer and set it in the refrigerator to thaw for tomorrow's dinner. Also, since the hard work of cutting up the meat has already been done, it's easy to cook up a dish.

None of this is hard. But it does take time and effort. When Steve and I worked fulltime, we did most of our cooking on the weekends. During the week we ate what we had prepared on weekends. It was worth our time and effort.

With your baggie of chicken in hand, you could cook any of these dishes from recipes in this cookbook:

- Chicken Parmesan Pasta Salad
- Stefano's Chicken Cacciatore
- Chicken Cordon Blue-Eyed Steve
- Chicken Baked in Steve's BBQ Sauce
- Curry Chicken Fingers
- Rosemary Coriander Chicken
- Chicken with Vegetables
- Curry Chicken with Vegetables
- Spicy Cornflake Chicken Bites
- Paprika Chicken
- Cinnamon and Cumin Chicken
- Chicken Soup with Pork Verde Broth

Creamy Chicken Casserole

*One evening, after making Scrumptious Scalloped Potatoes, I thought, "Hey, why not put **chicken** in this dish?" This is a mild dish, comfort food, for sure. You can use leftover cooked chicken or cook some up.*

> **2 medium potatoes (2 cups when cooked and sliced)**
> **2 Tbsps diced onion**
> **1/4 cup chopped mushrooms**
> **Olive oil**
> **1/2 lb raw chicken** *or* **1½ cups leftover cooked chicken, in pieces**
> **Curry powder, to taste**
> **Ground pepper, to taste: black, cayenne or white**
> **1/2 can of condensed cream of chicken soup (or cream of mushroom)**
> **1/3 cup milk**
> **1/3 cup shredded cheese (Sharp cheddar is good.)**
> **Paprika (or turmeric) for color**
> **Nonstick cooking oil spray**

- Boil potatoes in water until they're not quite done, about 25 minutes. Cut into slices. Set aside.
- Sauté the onions in olive oil, about 5 minutes. Set aside.
- Sauté the mushrooms in olive oil. Set aside.
- Cook chicken strips in a skillet with olive oil. (Skip this step if you're using leftover cooked chicken). Add in curry powder and pepper.
- In a bowl, mix cream of chicken soup with milk. Set aside in the refrigerator.
- Oil an 8" x 8" baking dish with nonstick cooking oil spray.
- Arrange the potato slices and chicken pieces in the baking dish.
- Add in mushrooms, onion, curry powder, and ground pepper.
- Pour in the cream of chicken soup mixture.
- Sprinkle cheese and paprika over the entire top.
- Bake uncovered at 350 degrees for about 30 minutes.

Serves 3.

Stefano's Easy Chicken Cacciatore

Chicken breasts or thighs, enough for 2 people
1/2 cup white wine
1½ to 2 cups marinara sauce:
- **From a jar** *or*
- leftover *Joey's Marinara* **(see recipe in This and That section)**

➢ Put chicken in a gallon-size baggie, pour in white wine, and place the baggie in the refrigerator for at least 20 minutes.
➢ Lift the chicken breasts out of baggie with a fork and place them in a baking dish.
➢ Pour marinara sauce over the chicken.
➢ Bake until chicken is done:
- *uncovered* at 350 degrees, for 45 to 60 minutes

or
- *tin-foil covered* at 375 degrees for an hour or slightly longer.

Serves 2.

Chicken Cordon Blue-Eyed Steve

Another delicious creation of Steve's. The chicken is not breaded, as traditional cordon bleu is. Basically this dish is baked chicken pieces with a slice of bacon or ham wrapped around each one.

2 boneless chicken thighs
6 turkey bacon slices or ham slices
1/4 cup diced mushrooms
2 to 4 Tbsps grated cheese (optional)
Ground black pepper, to taste
Parsley dried or fresh (for a nice presentation)

- Remove skin and bone from chicken thighs.
- Cut each chicken thigh into thirds.
- Wrap each chicken piece with a slice of bacon or ham. Place these in a shallow baking dish.
- Sprinkle on the mushrooms and black pepper.
- Bake at 350 degrees for about 1 hour.
- During the last 5 minutes, sprinkle on the cheese and parsley.

Serves 2.

Chicken Baked in Steve's BBQ Sauce

The beauty of this recipe is that it is simple, yet tastes delicious.

1½ lbs chicken: thighs, breasts, or legs
Steve's BBQ Sauce for Baking **(see recipe)**

- Get a baking dish and mix *Steve's Marinade for Baking* in it.
- Place the chicken in the baking dish.
- Bake at 350 degrees, uncovered, for 60 minutes.
- Approximately halfway through the bake time, turn each piece of chicken over.

Serves 4.

Note: This chicken dish is good with brown rice.

Steve's BBQ Sauce for Baking

1/4 cup white wine
1/4 cup BBQ sauce from a bottle
1/4 cup ketchup
1 Tbsp soy sauce
1 Tbsp + 1 tsp Dijon mustard
1 tsp Worcestershire sauce
1 tsp ground ginger
White pepper, to taste

➢ Mix all ingredients together and stir. You can mix it directly in the baking dish you'll be using.

Note: This sauce is good with chicken, pork, beef, and shrimp. (For beef you can use red wine instead of white.)

Curry Chicken Strips

1/2 lb raw chicken, cut into finger-size strips
1/4 cup white wine
1/4 cup olive oil
1/4 cup diced onion
2 Tbsps honey
2 Tbsps soy sauce
1 clove garlic, minced
Spices:
    1 Tbsp curry powder
    1 tsp ground coriander
    1 tsp ginger powder
    1/4 tsp cumin
    1/4 tsp ground cayenne pepper

- Place the chicken strips in a freezer baggie.
- In a bowl, make a marinade by mixing all of the other ingredients.
- Pour the marinade into the baggie of chicken. Refrigerate 20 minutes or longer.
- Pour the marinade and chicken into a skillet.
- Cook on medium heat, turning over occasionally, until chicken is done, 10 to 15 minutes.

Serves 2.

Do You Like that Rock?

An acquaintance of mine says she's interested in the correct pairing of herbs and spices. She doesn't want to combine two seasonings that will taste bad together. I know what she means. Recently, I put two spices together in a soup, and the broth tasted terrible. (I'm not saying which two spices in case they are somebody's favorite combo.) But Steve had a completely different experience; to him, the soup tasted good. People's palates and preferences obviously differ, and so it seems to me that pairing spices and herbs is a personal thing.

This reminds me of something that Ed, president of a gem and mineral club Steve and I once belonged to, said to us club members: "Do *you* like that rock? If so, it's a good rock."

Ed said it's not important what the *conventional thinking* is about a particular kind of rock. (For example, people think purple amethyst is "better" than white quartz.) He said it doesn't matter what *value* people attach to a gem. (For example, diamonds are more expensive than pearls.)

Ed drove home this point: The only thing that matters is what *you* think about the rock. If you like it, pick it up and keep it for your collection. If you don't like it, leave it on the ground. You, and you alone, determine what a good rock is.

Isn't it the same thing with herb and spice pairing? Do *you* like those two seasonings together? If so, it's a good pairing. That's all that matters.

Here's something much more important than spice pairing: *Be thankful you have something to eat and drink!* Never take nourishing food and clean water for granted. Be grateful, on a daily basis, for the sustenance that is available to you and your loved ones.

Rosemary Coriander Chicken

The cooking steps are the same as Curry Chicken Fingers; *the ingredients are different.*

1 lb raw chicken, cut into strips or pieces
1/4 cup white wine
2 Tbsps olive oil
1 to 2 Tbsps soy sauce (Depends on how salty you like your food.)
1 clove garlic, minced
Spices:
    1 tsp ground coriander
    1/2 tsp dried rosemary or a sprig of fresh rosemary
    1/4 tsp ground white pepper
    1/4 tsp salt

- Place the chicken strips in a freezer baggie.
- In a bowl, make a marinade by mixing all of the other ingredients.
- Pour the marinade into the baggie of chicken. Refrigerate 20 minutes or longer.
- Pour the marinade and chicken into a skillet.
- Cook on medium heat, turning over occasionally, until chicken is done, 10 to 15 minutes.

Serves 2.

Chicken Fried Rice

Great way to eat the leftovers in your refrigerator.

1/2 cup uncooked white rice *or* brown rice
**1/2 lb chicken (about 1 cup), raw or already cooked,
 cubed *or* cut into strips**
1 Tbsp canola oil *or* olive oil
1 tsp sesame seed oil
1/2 cup chopped onion

2 cups of vegetables, at least 3 kinds, cut up, such as:

mustard greens	snow peas	zucchini	celery
mushrooms	asparagus	broccoli	corn
bell pepper	bok choy	carrot	peas

1 Tbsp soy sauce
Sriracha sauce, to taste (or any other hot sauce you like)
Ground ginger
Ground white pepper, to taste
Nonstick cooking oil spray
1 egg, lightly beaten
1/3 cup diced ham
3 slices of firm tofu, soaked in soy sauce

➢ Cook the rice according to directions on the package. Set aside.
➢ Pour the oils into a large skillet and sauté the chicken and onion. (If using already-cooked chicken, no need to sauté it; instead add chicken in with the vegetables.)
➢ When chicken is almost done, add in the vegetables, soy sauce, and seasonings. Cook, partially covered, on medium-low, 5 minutes. Stir.
➢ In a corner of the skillet, spray nonstick cooking oil. Scramble the egg.
➢ Add in diced ham and tofu.
➢ Add in the rice, only as much as you want. (Or keep the rice separate.) Stir.

Serves 3.

Chicken with Vegetables over Rice

1/2 lb raw chicken (about 1 cup), cut into strips or cubes
1/4 cup white wine
1 Tbsp soy sauce
2/3 cup white rice *or* brown rice, uncooked
1/4 cup olive oil (divided)
1/4 cup chopped onion
2 cups of vegetables, at least 3 kinds, cut into bite sizes, such as:

mustard greens	lima beans	tomatoes	carrots
Napa cabbage	asparagus	broccoli	celery
bell pepper	snow peas	zucchini	chard
mushrooms	bok choy	broccoli	peas

Sriracha sauce and soy sauce, to top (optional)

- Put chicken, wine, and soy sauce in a baggie. Marinate in the refrigerator for 20 minutes or longer.
- Cook rice according to directions on the package. Set aside.
- In a skillet, sauté onions in 1 tablespoon of olive oil, about 5 minutes. Place onions in a small dish and set aside.
- In a separate skillet, dump the chicken and its marinade. Add in a tablespoon of olive oil. Cook, uncovered, on medium-low heat, turning frequently, until chicken is done, 5 to 15 minutes. (Cook time depends on size of chicken strips/cubes.)
- Meanwhile, to the "onion skillet" put in the vegetables and 2 tablespoons of olive oil. Add a little water, as needed. Cook, covered, on medium heat, 5 to 8 minutes.
- When the vegetables are done, add them and onions to the "chicken skillet." Stir. Heat on low until everything is piping hot.
- Serve over rice.
- Top with Sriracha sauce and soy sauce (both optional).

Serves 2.

Curry Chicken with Vegetables over Rice

Similar to Chicken with Vegetables *(previous recipe) except you add in spices.*

> **1/2 lb raw chicken (about 1 cup), cut into strips or cubes**
> **1/4 cup white wine**
> **1 Tbsp soy sauce**
> **2/3 cup white rice *or* brown rice, uncooked**
> **Spices, mixed together in a small bowl:**
> > **1½ tsps curry powder**
> > **1 tsp coriander**
> > **1/4 tsp each: cinnamon, clove, and cumin**
> > **1/16 tsp (or more) cayenne**
>
> **1/4 cup olive oil (divided)**
> **1/4 cup chopped onion**
> **2 cups of vegetables, at least 3 kinds, cut up, from list on**
> > ***Chicken with Vegetables Over Rice* recipe.**

- Put chicken, wine, and soy sauce in a baggie. Marinate in the refrigerator for 20 minutes or longer.
- Cook rice according to directions on the package. Set aside.
- In a skillet, sauté onions in 1 tablespoon of olive oil, about 5 minutes. Place onions in a small dish and set aside.
- In a separate skillet, dump the chicken and its marinade. Add in the bowl of spices and a tablespoon of olive oil. Cook, uncovered, on medium-low heat, turning frequently, until chicken is done, 5 to 15 minutes. (Cook time depends on size of chicken strips/cubes.)
- Meanwhile, to the "onion skillet" add the vegetables and 2 tablespoons of olive oil. Add a little water, as needed. Cook, covered, on medium heat, 5 to 8 minutes.
- When the vegetables are done, add them and onions to the "chicken skillet." Stir. Heat on low until everything is piping hot.
- Serve over rice. Top with soy sauce (optional).

Serves 2.

Spicy Cornflake Chicken Bites

We've written a lot of directions but it's simple, really: you dip chicken into cornflakes, add spices, and throw it in the oven. You'll need a cookie rack and a cookie sheet.

1 lb boneless, skinless chicken, cut in bite-size pieces or strips
1 cup milk
About 2 cups cornflakes
1/2 tsp poultry seasoning
1/2 tsp garlic salt
1/4 tsp salt
1/4 tsp white pepper (1/2 tsp if you like things spicy hot)
1/4 tsp cayenne pepper (1/2 tsp if you like things spicy hot)
Nonstick cooking spray oil

- Soak chicken in a bowl of milk for 30 to 60 minutes.
- Pour cornflakes onto a sheet of wax paper and crush them with a drinking glass, then pour them onto a dinner plate.
- In a small bowl, mix your spices. Set aside.
- Place a cookie sheet on top of a cookie rack. Spray both with nonstick cooking oil.
- Dip and mix a chicken piece in the cornflakes so that the cornflakes stick, then place it onto the cookie rack. Repeat with each chicken piece.
- Carefully, but liberally, spoon the spices over each piece of chicken.
- Lightly spray the cornflake-covered chicken with nonstick cooking oil.
- Bake at 350 degrees for 25 to 30 minutes.

Serves 4.

Paprika Chicken

For when you want things mild.

1 lb raw chicken cut into strips or pieces
Paprika (Use lots of it!)
Salt or garlic salt, to taste
Ground pepper, to taste: black, cayenne or white
Nonstick cooking oil spray

- Spray skillet with nonstick cooking oil.
- Cook chicken strips in a skillet on both sides for a few minutes, until not quite done.
- Remove any water from the skillet. (Some chicken has water added to it by the producer.)
- Season the chicken strips with salt, pepper, and lots of paprika.
- Cook until chicken is done, 10 to 15 minutes, turning over a few times.

Serves 2.

Cinnamon & Cumin Chicken

Recipe is the same as Paprika Chicken *except you omit the paprika and add in cinnamon and cumin.*

> **1 lb raw chicken cut into strips or pieces**
> **Cinnamon, to taste**
> **Cumin, to taste**
> **Salt or garlic salt, to taste**
> **Ground pepper, to taste: black, cayenne or white**
> **Nonstick cooking oil spray**

- Spray skillet with nonstick cooking oil.
- Cook chicken strips in a skillet on both sides for a few minutes.
- Remove any water from the skillet. (Some chicken has water added to it by the producer.)
- Sprinkle spices on the chicken strips, both sides.
- Cook until chicken is done, 10 to 15 minutes, turning over a few times.

Serves 2.

Chicken Enchilada Casserole

1 lb (2 cups, cubed) already-cooked chicken*
10 oz can red enchilada sauce
8 to 10 corn tortillas
16 oz can refried beans
1 can (4 oz) Ortega chilies
1 cup grated sharp cheddar cheese
Nonstick cooking oil spray

- Set aside your chicken.
- Spray nonstick cooking oil into an 8 x 11 inch baking dish. Set aside.
- Pour some of the enchilada sauce onto a dinner plate.
- Dip each tortilla into the enchilada sauce and lay them in the baking dish. You may want to cut some of the tortillas in half so they fit better.
- Layer the other ingredients on top of the tortillas in this order:
    - Refried beans
    - Green chilies
    - Chicken
    - the remaining enchilada sauce
    - Cheese
- Cover baking dish with aluminum foil.
- Bake at 350 degrees for 35 minutes.
- At the 20-minute mark, remove foil and bake uncovered 15 more minutes.

Serves 4.

Note: *You can use chicken from leftover *Chicken-in-a-Pot*.

Steve's Moist Herbed Thanksgiving Turkey

Turkey doesn't have to be just for Thanksgiving; it's fun to bake a turkey mid-year. Steve pours oil and herbs under the skin at the beginning, which eliminates the need to open the oven and baste the turkey every half hour. Amounts are "to taste."

Whole turkey or turkey breast
Poultry seasoning
Garlic salt
White pepper
White wine
Olive oil
You'll need aluminum foil, a large oven tray, and a broiler pan.

<u>Preparing the turkey</u>
- Mix seasonings, wine, and oil in a small bowl.
- Wash the turkey and remove the inside packet.
- Put your hand in between the skin and meat and lift up, then pour or spoon in the seasoned wine mixture.
- On the outside of the turkey, pour olive oil and seasonings.

<u>Baking the turkey</u>
- Preheat oven according to the instructions on the turkey wrapper.
- Place the broiler pan on the tray and pour water into the tray.
- Set turkey on the broiler pan.
- Make an aluminum tent for the turkey.
- Bake turkey for the time recommended on the turkey wrapper.
- Every so often add more water to the tray.
- Remove the tent during the last half hour of baking.

<u>Out of the oven</u>
- Set the turkey on the counter for 20 minutes before slicing it. This way the juices absorb into the meat.

Pork

Sweet and Sour Pork over Rice

2 thin pork chops or 1/2 lb country ribs—in chunks or thin strips
2/3 cup uncooked brown rice
1 Tbsp olive oil
1/2 tsp ground ginger
Ground cayenne, to taste
2 Tbsps cornstarch and 2 Tbsps cold water

2 cups (or more) vegetables, at least 3 kinds, cut up, such as:

carrot, shredded	cauliflower	asparagus	celery
mustard greens	bell pepper	bok choy	corn
green beans	snow peas	broccoli	peas

1 cup chicken broth
2 Tbsps soy sauce   1/2 cup onion, chopped*
2 Tbsps vinegar   1/2 cup pineapple, in chunks*
1 Tbsp sugar   2 Tbsps pimiento, chopped*
1 cup mushrooms, sliced   2 slices of firm tofu, cubed*

➢ Cook the rice according to directions on the package, then set aside.
➢ In a large skillet, cook pork in olive oil, ginger, and cayenne, on medium heat, tossing frequently, about 5 minutes.
➢ Mix 2 tablespoons each of cornstarch and cold water in a cup. Set aside.
➢ When the pork is almost done, add in vegetables, pineapple, chicken broth, soy sauce, vinegar, and sugar. Bring to boil, then reduce heat to medium-low and cook about 3 minutes.
➢ Add in cornstarch water, a spoonful at a time, stirring constantly. Sauce will thicken as mixture bubbles. Use only the amount you need.
➢ Add in tofu.
➢ Serve over rice.

Serves 2 or 3.

Note: * = Optional ingredient

Verde Valley Pork Verde
(in a Slow Cooker)

2 lbs pork (shoulder, loin, or chops)
   with fat and tendons removed, cut in chunks
28 oz can of green chile enchilada sauce
1 medium onion, chopped
1/2 cup white wine
3 carrots, sliced
3 celery stalks, sliced

➢ Place all ingredients in a slow cooker and cook until meat is tender. Refer to manufacturer's instructions as to how long to cook; our cook time is about 6 hours but slow cookers vary.
➢ Serve in bowls over rice or cubed boiled potatoes. Or serve with tortillas on the side.

Serves 6.

Notes:
- Put the leftovers in separate containers: 1) verde broth *with* pork and 2) verde broth *without* pork. Label and place in your freezer and/or refrigerator.
- What do you do with the verde broth *without* pork? You make *Chicken in Pork Verde Broth* (see next recipe). Basically, on another day, you make a quick soup.

Chicken in Pork Verde Broth
(A soup from leftover Pork Verde)

This is a soup and it has chicken in it—and yet it's in the Pork section. Why is it here? Reason is you make this soup from leftover Pork Verde, the previous recipe. No need to add seasonings because they are already in the broth.

> **1 cup raw chicken, cut in bite sizes***
> **1 Tbsp olive oil**
> **2 cups leftover Pork Verde broth**
> **1 cup (or more) vegetables, diced—any kind**
>
> **Tortillas on the side (optional)**

- Sauté the chicken in olive oil.
- Meanwhile, put the Pork Verde broth in a saucepan, add the vegetables, and heat on medium.
- When the chicken is done, add it to the soup.
- Serve with tortillas on the side.

Serves 2.

Notes:
*Perhaps you have chicken in a baggie in your freezer inventory. (More on inventory in *An Easier Tomorrow,* near the beginning of the Poultry section.)
*Actually, chicken is optional.

Boneless Country Ribs, Marinated and Baked

Steve bakes country ribs two different ways. The first way is to marinate the pork for an hour and then bake it (see recipe this page). The second way is to parboil the pork and then bake it (see recipe on next page). Both recipes use Steve's BBQ Sauce for Baking.

1½ lbs boneless pork country ribs, cut in large chunks
***Steve's BBQ Sauce for Baking* (see recipe)**

- Put meat in a gallon-size baggie.
- Pour *Steve's BBQ Sauce for Baking* (see recipe) into the baggie *or* make the sauce right in the baggie.
- Let marinate for about 1 hour.
- Put both pork and marinade in a baking dish.
- Cover baking dish with aluminum foil.
- Bake at 325 degrees for about 1½ hours.

Serves 4.

Note: With leftovers, make *Pork Fried Rice* (see recipe in this section).

Boneless Country Ribs, Parboiled and Baked

Steve prefers this method over the one-hour-marinade-and-bake method (previous recipe) because the fat is boiled out.

> **1½ lbs boneless pork country ribs cut in large chunks**
> **1/4 cup olive oil**
> **Garlic salt, to taste**
> **Ground ginger, to taste**
> **2 bay leaves**
> **White pepper, to taste**
> ***Steve's BBQ Sauce for Baking* (see recipe)**

➢ Parboil the meat:
  o Place pork in boiling water along with olive oil, garlic salt, ginger, bay leaves, and white pepper.
  o Bring back to boil and then reduce heat to low.
  o Cook, covered, for 45 minutes.
➢ Afterwards, pork may be placed in refrigerator to be baked later *or* bake it now.
➢ Put pork in a baking dish and pour *Steve's BBQ Sauce for Baking* (see recipe) over it *or* make the sauce directly in the baking dish.
➢ Cover baking dish with aluminum foil.
➢ Bake at 300 degrees for 45 minutes.

Serves 4.

Note: With leftovers, make *Pork Fried Rice* (see recipe in this section).

Steve's BBQ Sauce for Baking

This recipe also appears in the Poultry section. For convenience, I'm also placing it here.

- **1/4 cup white wine**
- **1/4 cup BBQ sauce from a bottle**
- **1/4 cup ketchup**
- **1 Tbsp soy sauce**
- **2 Tbsps Dijon mustard**
- **1 tsp Worcestershire sauce**
- **1 tsp ground ginger**
- **White pepper, to taste**

➢ Mix all ingredients together and stir. You can mix it directly in a gallon-size baggie containing the meat *or* in the baking dish you'll be using.

Note: This sauce is good with chicken, pork, beef, and shrimp. For beef you can use red wine instead of white.

Steve's Pork Roast

When Steve cooks a pork roast, he marinates the meat for at least an hour before putting meat and marinade in the oven.

> **1½ lbs pork: shoulder, loin, or butt**
> ***Steve's Marinade for Pork* (see recipe)**

- Cut a few slits in the roast (so that the marinade can penetrate).
- In a gallon-size baggie, marinate the pork in *Steve's Marinade for Pork* (see recipe) for an hour or longer.
- Place the pork in a baking dish.
- Pour the marinade over the pork.
- Bake at 350 degrees for 40 to 45 minutes (although it really depends on the shape of your roast and how thick it is).
- Check at 40 minutes. If not done, put it back in the oven and monitor.

Serves 4.

Note: With leftovers, make *Pork Fried Rice* (see recipe in this section).

Steve's Marinade for Pork

This is the marinade recipe for Steve's Pork Roast. *(It is very similar to* Steve's BBQ Sauce for Baking.) *He lets the marinade work on the pork for an hour or longer in the refrigerator. He includes (pours) this marinade in the baking dish.*

<u>Marinade for pork</u>
1/2 cup white wine
2 Tbsps olive oil
1 Tbsp soy sauce
1 Tbsp + 1 tsp Dijon mustard
2 tsps Worcestershire sauce
1/2 tsp Italian seasonings
1/2 tsp sage
Garlic salt, to taste
Black pepper, to taste

- In a small bowl, mix together all ingredients *except* the seasonings.
- Put the pork in a gallon-size baggie.
- Pour the marinade into the baggie.
- Add in the seasonings: Italian, sage, garlic salt, and pepper.
- Seal the baggie and place in your refrigerator for an hour or longer.
- Include this marinade in the baking dish when baking the pork.

Pork Roast with Fruit

1½ lbs pork: shoulder, loin, or butt
1/4 cup white wine
2 Tbsps lemon juice (optional)
1/2 cup fresh apple, diced*
1/4 cup raisins**
Sage, to taste
Allspice, to taste
Clove, to taste
Nutmeg, to taste

- Cut a 3" slit in the pork roast.
- In a gallon-size baggie, marinate the pork in wine and lemon juice for 1 to 2 hours.
- Place the pork and marinade in a baking dish.
- Stuff the fruit inside the slit you made in the roast.
- Sprinkle seasonings over the pork.
- Cover the baking dish with aluminum foil.
- Bake at 350 degrees for about 1 hour.

Serves 4.

Notes:
*Instead of apple, you can use pineapple.
**Instead of raisins, you can use dried apricots, cranberries, figs, or a combo. Or six prunes (I tried more and it was too many).

Pork Fried Rice

1/2 cup uncooked white rice *or* brown rice
1 to 2 cups cubed pork, raw or already cooked*
1 Tbsp canola oil and 1 tsp sesame seed oil
1/2 cup chopped onion
2 cups of vegetables, at least 3 kinds, cut up, such as:

mustard greens	cauliflower	bok choy	celery
yellow squash	bell pepper	zucchini	kale
green beans	asparagus	broccoli	corn
mushrooms	snow peas	carrots	peas

1 Tbsp soy sauce
Sriracha sauce, to taste
Ground ginger, to taste
Ground white pepper, to taste
Nonstick cooking oil spray
1 egg, lightly beaten
3 slices of firm tofu, soaked in soy sauce

➢ Cook rice according to directions on the package. Set aside.
➢ Pour the oils into a large skillet and sauté the pork and onion. (If using already-cooked pork, no need to sauté it; instead add pork in with the vegetables.)
➢ When pork is almost done, add in vegetables, soy sauce, and seasonings. Cook, partially covered, on medium-low, 5 minutes. Stir.
➢ In a corner of the skillet, spray nonstick cooking oil. Scramble the egg.
➢ Add in the rice, only as much as you want. (Or keep the rice separate.) Stir.

Serves 3.

> Note: *Use pork chops or boneless country ribs. You can also use chicken, beef, shrimp, tofu, or a combo.

Pork with Vegetables over Rice

**1/2 lb (about 1 cup) pork chops or boneless country ribs,
   cut into strips or cubes**
1/4 cup white wine
1 Tbsp soy sauce
2/3 cup white rice *or* brown rice, uncooked
1/4 cup olive oil (divided)
1/4 cup chopped onion
2 cups of vegetables, at least 3 kinds, cut into bite sizes, such as:

mustard greens	lima beans	tomatoes	carrots
Napa cabbage	asparagus	broccoli	celery
bell pepper	snow peas	zucchini	chard
mushrooms	bok choy	broccoli	peas

Sriracha sauce and soy sauce, to top (optional)

- Put pork, wine, and soy sauce in a baggie. Marinate in the refrigerator for 20 minutes or longer.
- Cook rice according to directions on the package. Set aside.
- In a skillet, sauté onions in 1 tablespoon of olive oil, about 5 minutes. Place onions in a small dish and set aside.
- In a separate skillet, dump the pork and its marinade. Add in a tablespoon of olive oil. Cook, uncovered, on medium-low heat, turning frequently, until pork is done, 5 to 15 minutes. (Cook time depends on size of pork strips/cubes.)
- Meanwhile, to the "onion skillet" put in the vegetables and 2 tablespoons of olive oil. Add a little water, as needed. Cook, covered, on medium heat, 5 to 8 minutes.
- When the vegetables are done, add them and onions to the "pork skillet." Stir. Heat on low until everything is piping hot.
- Serve over rice.
- Top with Sriracha sauce and soy sauce (both optional).

Serves 2.

Curry Pork with Vegetables over Rice

Similar to Pork with Vegetables *(previous recipe) except you add in spices.*

>**1/2 lb (about 1 cup) pork chops or boneless country ribs,
>   cut into strips or cubes
>1/4 cup white wine
>1 Tbsp soy sauce
>2/3 cup white rice *or* brown rice, uncooked
>Spices, mixed together in a small bowl:
>   1½ tsps curry powder
>   1 tsp coriander
>   1/4 tsp each: cinnamon, clove, and cumin
>   1/16 tsp (or more) cayenne 1/4 cup olive oil (divided)
>1/4 cup chopped onion
>2 cups of vegetables, at least 3 kinds, cut up, from list on
>   *Pork with Vegetables* recipe.**

- Put pork, wine, and soy sauce in a baggie. Marinate in the refrigerator for 20 minutes or longer.
- Cook rice according to directions on the package. Set aside.
- In a skillet, sauté onions in 1 tablespoon of olive oil, about 5 minutes. Place onions in a small dish and set aside.
- In a separate skillet, dump the pork and its marinade. Add in the bowl of spices and a tablespoon of olive oil. Cook, uncovered, on medium-low heat, turning frequently, until pork is done, 5 to 15 minutes. (Cook time depends on size of pork strips/cubes.)
- Meanwhile, to the "onion skillet" add the vegetables and 2 tablespoons of olive oil. Add a little water. Cook, covered, on medium heat, 5 to 8 minutes.
- When the vegetables are done, add them and onions to the "pork skillet." Stir. Heat on low until everything is piping hot.
- Serve over rice. Top with soy sauce (optional).

Serves 2.

Beef

California Pot Roast

Steve learned to make pot roast from his mom. Like my mother, Steve's mom stretched the food budget by purchasing an inexpensive cut of meat and slow-cooked it till it was tender. Steve walked me through this recipe. I call it California Pot Roast *because of the generous amount of California red wine he uses. This dish needs 4 to 5 hours to cook over the stove. The aromas are going to drive you crazy.*

3 lbs boneless beef shoulder
3 cloves garlic, diced
2 Tbsps olive oil
Salt, to taste
Ground black pepper, to taste
3 to 4 cups beef broth*
1 cup red wine
2 or 3 bay leaves
1 tsp Italian seasonings
1 onion, chopped
1 cup chopped mushrooms
Egg noodles

- Sauté diced garlic and olive oil in a large pot, 5 minutes.
- Set the beef in the pot, salt and pepper it, and sear it on medium heat, 10 minutes on each side, a total of 20 minutes.
- Add in the beef broth, wine, seasonings, onion, and mushrooms. Bring to a boil, then reduce heat to low (gentle bubble). Cook with the lid on for **4 to 5 hours** on your stovetop.
- About 15 or 20 minutes before serving, cook the egg noodles (separately).
- Serve in bowls, over egg noodles.

Serves 6 to 10.   (Continued on next page)

California Pot Roast
(Page 2)

Notes:
*Use two 14 oz cans of beef broth *or* one 32 oz box.

You'll have some wonderful pot likker from this dish, i.e., the left-behind liquid from boiling meat. From the pot likker you can make soups from recipes in this cookbook:
- *Shelly's Borscht*
- *Hamburger Soup*
- *Beef Vegetable Soup*
- *Tomato Vegetable Stew*

From the leftover beef you can make:
- beef *Tacos* (see recipe)
- beef *Enchilada Casserole* (see recipe),
- beef burritos
- pot roast sandwiches

Put the leftovers in containers. Label them. Place one in your refrigerator and the rest in your freezer. Inventory!

Steve's Beef Stew (in a Slow Cooker)

*Steve marinates the beef for **a day or two** (!) before cooking this dish. (See* Steve's Beef Marinade *recipe.)*

    **1½ to 2 lbs cubed boneless beef roast,
        such as rump roast, shoulder roast, or London Broil
    One 14 oz can beef broth
    1/2 cup red wine
    2 bay leaves
    1 to 2 cups cubed potato, yam, turnip or a combo
    1 small onion, chopped
    2 carrots, sliced (optional)
    2 celery stalks, sliced (optional)
    About 6 mushrooms, sliced (optional)**

- Marinate the beef for **one to two days** using *Steve's Marinade for Beef* recipe.
- After a day or two has passed, get your slow cooker out and place the meat *and its marinade* inside the slow cooker.
- During the last hour or two, add in the potatoes. The vegetables can also be added *or* steam them separately.)
- Slow cookers vary in cook time; see your manufacturer's recommendations.

Serves 6.

Note: When we eat leftover *Beef Stew*, sometimes we add in a couple new veggies—such as cabbage, cauliflower, corn, green beans, yellow squash, or zucchini—to perk up the dish.

Steve's Marinade for Beef Stew and Chili

*This is the marinade recipe Steve uses to ready **beef** for chili or stew (see recipes for* Steve's Beef Chili *and* Steve's Beef Stew*). He lets the marinade work on the beef for **a day or two in the refrigerator**. He says it's mainly about the red wine tenderizing the meat.*

<u>Marinade for *beef*</u>:
1/2 cup *red* wine
2 Tbsps olive oil
1 Tbsp soy sauce
1 tsp Worcestershire sauce
1/2 tsp Italian seasonings
1/2 tsp sage
Garlic salt, to taste
Black pepper, to taste

- In a large bowl, mix all of the ingredients together.
- Put the cubed beef in a gallon-size baggie.
- Pour the marinade into the baggie.
- Seal and place in your refrigerator for **a day or two**.
- When you begin making your chili or stew, *do* include this marinade in the pot!

What is Chili?

People get emotional about what chili is, and they will passionately defend their position. A few years ago, I unwittingly found myself in such a discussion. Whew!

Before I go further, I want to clarify something. When I say "chili" I am referring to a dish, specifically a *stew*. I'm not talking about a spice. If I were talking about chili as a spice or the actual chili fruit, I would say "chili powder" or "chili peppers" or "diced chilies."

The main argument surrounding chili is whether or not it contains *beans*. Some folks insist, "Absolutely no beans!" while others say, "Of course chili has beans!"

Another argument around chili is *tradition*. I agree that it's good to use an old chili recipe; keep history alive. However, humans are *creative* and they naturally change things. You can't prevent creativity. Also, people want *variation* in their diet and will cook things in a new way to achieve variety. *Supply and demand* come into the picture, too, affecting recipes as ingredients become scare or abundant, expensive or cheap. My point is that recipes naturally evolve, and while some folks may stick to their traditional chili recipe, others are going to change it up.

When it comes to chili, Cody uses no beans, while Jody always includes them. Joann dislikes tomatoes; Leeann adores them. Alice insists that fresh chili peppers must be used; Dallas says, "I use chili *powder*." Ben insists, "Chili must have heat" while Jen says, "Don't burn my mouth!" It gets down to one's individual preference. Everybody's right and nobody's wrong.

Here's the thing: *chili can be made in an endless number of ways and you should always make it the way YOU like it.*

Beef

Steve's Beef Chili (in a Slow Cooker)

*Steve marinates the beef for **a day or two** before cooking chili (see* Steve's Beef Marinade *recipe).*

    1½ to 2 lbs cubed boneless beef roast* and its marinade
    1 can (14 oz) beef broth
    1 can (14 oz) diced tomatoes
    1/2 cup red wine
    1 onion, chopped
    1/2 cup chili powder

- Marinate the beef for **one to two days** using *Steve's Beef Marinade* recipe.
- After a day or two has passed, get your slow cooker out and place the meat *and its marinade* inside the slow cooker.
- Add in all of the other ingredients.
- Cook the beef in the slow cooker. Slow cookers vary in cook time; see your manufacturer's recommendations.

Serves 6.

Notes:
- *Any cut of beef will do: rump roast, shoulder roast, London broil.
- *You can also use a pork roast (loin, shoulder, butt) instead of beef.
- Optional: add a 14 oz can (or just a cup) of white beans or kidney beans.
- Leftovers? How about *Beef Chili Vegetable Soup* recipe (next recipe) for a quick and simple soup.

Beef Chili Vegetable Soup

This is a soup—*and yet it's in the Beef section. Why? You make it from leftover* Steve's Beef Chili *and I thought it naturally followed that recipe. No need to add seasonings because they are already in the broth. As for veggies, just choose a few from this list.*

2 cups leftover *Steve's Beef Chili** (see recipe). Just dip in and use whatever you have left over.

2 cups of vegetables, several kinds, cut into bite sizes, such as:

yellow squash	mushrooms	parsnip	turnip
green beans	lima beans	spinach	celery
bell pepper	tomatoes	hominy	corn
cauliflower	zucchini	carrot	peas

1/2 cup canned beans, any kind (optional)

➢ Combine all ingredients in a soup pot.
➢ Cook, covered, on low heat, until vegetables are done, about 10 minutes.

Serves 2.

Seasoned Ground Beef

1 Tbsp olive oil
1 clove garlic, minced (optional)
1/2 cup (or more) chopped onion
1 lb lean ground beef
Salt, to taste
Ground pepper, to taste

➢ Pour olive oil in a large soup pot or skillet and turn stove heat to medium.
➢ Sauté garlic, about 5 minutes.
➢ Add in the onion, ground beef, and seasonings. Chop beef up with a large spoon.
➢ Cook beef mixture on medium heat, stirring occasionally, until it is done, 8 to 10 minutes.
➢ Drain beef from skillet, if needed.

Serves 4.

Note: *Seasoned Ground Beef* freezes well.

What can you do with *Seasoned Ground Beef*? You can use it in these dishes:

Soup section:
    Add to *Magic Minestrone*
    Add to *Tomato Vegetable Stew*
    Add to *Shelly's Borscht*
    Hamburger Soup

Poultry section:
    Turkey Spaghetti recipe but use ground beef instead of ground turkey.

(Continued on next page)

Seasoned Ground Beef ideas, continued

Beef section:
    Shepherd's Pie
    Enchilada Casserole
    Steve's Favorite School Lunch

Warm Vegetables section:
    A Potato for Dawn
    Add to *Scrumptious Scalloped Potatoes*

This and That section:
    Tacos
    Add to *Joey's Marinara Sauce*
    Spaghetti Stretcher

Breakfast section:
    Add to *Steve's Breakfast Special*
    Add to *Home-fries for Dawn*

Steve's Favorite School Lunch

Of all the lunches he ate at school, Steve says this lunch was the one he looked forward to the most. (We jazzed it up a little bit with wine and mushrooms.)

> **2 or 3 small potatoes**
> 2/3 cup beef broth
> 1 tsp (or more) Worcestershire Sauce
> 1 tsp (or more) soy sauce
> 1 Tbsp (or more) red wine
> 1 Tbsp cornstarch
> 1 cup diced mushrooms
> 1 Tbsp olive oil
> 1/2 lb *Seasoned Ground Beef* (see recipe)

- Place potatoes in boiling water (skins on) and boil until done, about 25 minutes. Drain and leave them in the pot. Set aside.
- Meanwhile, mix all liquid ingredients in a bowl, and stir in cornstarch. Set aside.
- Sauté mushrooms in a tablespoon of olive oil. Set aside.
- Put *Seasoned Ground Beef* in a skillet. Add in the broth mixture and sautéed mushrooms. Stir and heat until broth thickens.
- Make lumpy mashed potatoes: in the pot they were boiled in, push potatoes down with a fork a few times.
- Plop potatoes onto individual plates and scoop beef mixture on top.

Serves 2.

Our Down-home Meatloaf

16 buttery round crackers
2 eggs
1/2 cup diced onion
1/2 cup shredded carrot
1/4 cup sliced celery
1/3 cup ketchup
1 Tbsp BBQ sauce (plus more for optional topping)
2 tsps Worcestershire Sauce
Ground white pepper, to taste
1 lb lean ground beef
Nonstick cooking oil spray

- Crush crackers by rolling a jar over them, either on wax paper or directly on your kitchen counter. Set aside.
- In a large bowl, lightly beat 2 eggs.
- Stir in onion, carrot, celery, ketchup, BBQ sauce, and Worcestershire Sauce.
- Mix in the ground beef. (I use a large spoon.)
- Mix in the crackers.
- Spray nonstick cooking oil into an 8" x 8" baking dish,* then spoon in mixture, spreading evenly.
- Bake at 350 degrees for 50 to 60 minutes.
- Top with BBQ sauce (optional).

Serves 4.

Notes:
- *To reduce bake time, use a baking dish instead of a loaf pan.
- This meatloaf recipe is a fusion of three recipes: my mom's, Steve's, and mine.
- Leftover ideas: tacos, burritos, sandwiches, pizza, or add it to marinara sauce (see *Joey's Marinara* in This and That section).

Swedish Meatballs

After trying various ingredients and amounts, Steve has come up with this recipe. Great taste and texture!

1/2 cup ground crackers, any kind
1/8 tsp ground white pepper
1/8 tsp ground black pepper
1/3 cup diced onion
2 tsps olive oil (to sauté)
2 eggs
1/3 cup ketchup
2 Tbsps BBQ sauce
1 lb lean ground beef
Nonstick cooking oil spray

- Crush crackers: put them on a cutting board and roll a tall water glass over them.
- In a small bowl, mix crushed crackers with white and black pepper. Set aside.
- Sauté onion in a skillet with olive oil. Set aside.
- In a large bowl, lightly beat eggs.
- Add to the large bowl: onions, ketchup, BBQ sauce, beef, and crackers. Mix well.
- Form into meatballs, 10 to 20, depending on the size you want.
- Spray nonstick cooking oil into a skillet.
- Fry as you would a burger, except roll/scrape the meatballs frequently, careful that they not break apart.

Serves 6. Makes 10 to 20 meatballs, depending on their size.

Notes:
- Place the leftover meatballs in freezer baggies and store in your freezer—they'll be ready anytime you want to defrost them. Inventory!
- With leftovers, make a burrito: Chopped meatball, refried beans, and Sriracha sauce in a flour tortilla.

Shepherd's Pie

3 medium potatoes
1 clove minced garlic (optional)
2 tsps olive oil
1/2 lb lean ground beef
1/2 cup diced onion
2 tsps Worcestershire Sauce
Ground pepper, to taste: black, cayenne or white
Salt, to taste: garlic, table or seasoned
3/4 cup canned green beans
1/2 cup canned corn
2 Tbsps diced: marinated pimiento (from a jar or can) *or*
 fresh red bell pepper *or*
 sun-dried tomatoes
1 cup shredded cheese (Jack, cheddar, and parmesan are good.)
Nonstick cooking spray oil

- Wash the potatoes, then boil them—skins on—about 30 minutes.
- Meanwhile, sauté the garlic in olive oil in a skillet.
- To the skillet, add in ground beef, onion, Worcestershire Sauce, salt, and pepper. Cook on medium heat.
- When the potatoes are done, mash them. (The skins will slough off; decide if you want to keep skins or discard them.) Sprinkle with salt and mix.
- Oil an 8 x 8 inch baking dish with nonstick cooking oil spray.
- Layer everything in baking dish in this order:
  - mashed potatoes on the bottom
  - ground beef with onions
  - vegetables
  - another layer of mashed potatoes
  - cheese on top
- Bake at 350 degrees for about 30 minutes.

Serves 4 to 5.

Beef Enchilada Casserole

1/2 lb *Seasoned Ground Beef* **(see recipe in Beef section)**
1 can (10 oz) red enchilada sauce
8 to 10 corn tortillas
1 can (16 oz) refried beans
1 can (4 oz) Ortega chilies
1 cup grated sharp cheddar cheese
Nonstick cooking oil spray

- Set aside your *Seasoned Ground Beef.*
- Spray nonstick cooking oil into an 8 x 11 inch baking dish. Set aside.
- Pour some of the enchilada sauce onto a dinner plate.
- Dip each tortilla into the enchilada sauce and lay them in the baking dish. You may want to cut some of the tortillas in half so they fit better in the baking dish.
- Layer the other ingredients on top of the tortillas in this order:
    - Refried beans
    - Green chilies
    - *Seasoned Ground Beef*
    - the remaining enchilada sauce
    - Cheese
- Cover baking dish with aluminum foil.
- Bake at 350 degrees for 35 minutes.
- At the 20-minute mark, remove foil and bake uncovered 15 more minutes.

Serves 4.

Idea: You can make enchiladas instead of this casserole using the same ingredients. Steps: Fill 2 tortillas with beef, beans, chilies, and cheese. Fold and place in oiled baking dish. Hold together with toothpicks. Make about 5 enchiladas. Pour enchilada sauce over the tops of the enchiladas.

Warm Vegetables

Byron's Brussels Sprouts

Byron is an elderly gentleman and World War II vet I met in Big Timber, Montana. He is friendly, the kind of person you feel like you've known all your life, the kind of person everybody likes. I loved to sit with him in the back row of church—knowing full-well his phone would ring midway through the sermon and that the pastor would give him "a look" and that I would stare at the stained glass so I wouldn't burst out laughing. (The pastor and I would chuckle about it later.) Byron has held a wide variety of jobs, including copper mining worker, fly-fishing guide, and grocery store owner. He gave me this recipe, and I assure you these Brussels sprouts taste better than the plain, boiled ones I had when I was a little sprout (see story in Crepes and Coyotes and Other Tales). *The amounts are up to you.*

Brussels sprouts
Olive oil*
Basil and/or thyme
Garlic salt or table salt
Ground pepper: black, cayenne or white

➢ Steam the Brussels sprouts for about 5 minutes.
➢ Transfer them to a saucepan—the bottom saucepan of your steamer set is ideal.
➢ Drizzle on olive oil, sprinkle on seasonings and sauté on medium heat, stirring frequently, until the vegetables are done, about 5 minutes.

Notes:
- *You could use butter instead of olive oil.
- You could actually substitute in any variety of veggies: carrots, zucchini, bok choy, mustard greens, etc.

Warm German-American Potatoes

This is our version of Hot German Potato Salad. *(Steve and I are both German American.) It is reminiscent of the dish my grandma served when I was a girl and was probably cooked by our ancestors for many generations. (See my story "Hot German Potato Salad in L.A." in* Crepes and Coyotes and Other Tales.*)*

2 or 3 red potatoes
1 Tbsp olive oil
2 Tbsps onion, minced
1/4 cup celery, diced
2 slices turkey bacon, chopped
2 Tbsps capers
1 tsp caper juice (from jar)
2 to 3 tsps apple cider vinegar
1/2 tsp dill
2 Tbsps plain yogurt
Ground black pepper, to taste

- Wash potatoes and then boil them in water, skins on, about 25 minutes.
- In a saucepan, sauté onion in olive oil, about 7 minutes.
- To the sauce pan add: celery, turkey bacon, capers, and caper juice. Heat on low, about 3 minutes.
- When potatoes are done, place them in a large bowl. Mash them with their skins on (just a few pushes with a masher). Lumps are okay.
- To the mashed potatoes add: vinegar, dill, yogurt, and pepper. Also add the celery/bacon mixture from the saucepan. Stir until blended.
- Taste and make sure you have the right amount of oil and vinegar for *you*.
- Serve warm; reheat in microwave if necessary.

Serves 2.

A Potato for Dawn

No quantities are given; it depends on the size of your potato and your personal taste. There's a story behind the name of this recipe. Dawn, through her example, challenged some notions I held and helped me to become a better person. (See "It's Surprising What You Can Do with a Potato" in Crepes and Coyotes and Other Tales.*)*

Potato, the size you want
Cooked meat, such as:
    Seasoned Ground Beef **(see recipe)**
    leftover chicken from ***Chicken-in-a-Pot*** **(see recipe)**
    sausage
    ham
Shredded cheese
Fresh tomatoes, chopped
Diced onions, raw or sautéed
Diced mushrooms, raw or sautéed
Salt, to taste
Ground pepper, to taste

- Bake your potato. Or parboil your potato and then microwave it.
- Split the potato lengthwise and then cut and separate the flesh, making space for the other ingredients.
- Fill the potato with meat, cheese, and veggies. Sprinkle on seasonings.
- Heat the filled potato in the microwave until the cheese melts.
- Be thankful you have something to eat.

Serves 1.

Note: You may be interested in a similar recipe, *Home-fries for Dawn* (in the Breakfast section).

Scrumptious Scalloped Potatoes

This is my mom's recipe with onions and mushrooms thrown in. I found it on a recipe card my sister June gave me decades ago. I remember eating those scalloped potatoes like it was yesterday. Everybody loves Dee's scalloped potatoes! Thanks, Mom!

4 to 5 small potatoes
1/3 cup diced onion
1 tsp olive oil
1 can (10.5 oz) condensed cream of mushroom soup
2/3 cup milk (about half of the soup can)
1/2 cup chopped mushrooms
Ground pepper, to taste: white, cayenne or black
1 cup grated cheese: cheddar, parmesan, mozzarella, Jack
Paprika, for color
Nonstick cooking oil spray

- Boil potatoes in water for 20 to 25 minutes, until they're not quite done. Cool. Cut into slices. Set aside.
- Sauté the onions in a teaspoon of olive oil. (This is an optional step; you can put *raw* diced onions directly into the baking dish.)
- In a bowl, mix the mushroom soup with the milk. Set aside in the refrigerator.
- Oil a baking dish with nonstick cooking oil spray.
- Arrange the potato slices in the baking dish.
- Sprinkle mushrooms, onion, and ground pepper over the potatoes.
- Pour in the mushroom soup mixture.
- Sprinkle on the cheese.
- Sprinkle paprika over the entire top.
- Bake uncovered at 350 degrees for 30 to 35 minutes.

Serves 4 or 5.

Skillet Eggplant with Zucchini and Mushrooms

Give the raw eggplant a salty soak to remove its bitterness.

2 cups eggplant, cubed or sliced **1/4 cup onions, diced***
2 teaspoons salt **1 cup mushrooms, sliced***
1 quart cold water **1 cup zucchini, sliced***
Olive oil, a little or a lot **Ground black pepper, to taste**
Shredded cheese to top: parmesan or mozzarella (optional)

Soak cut-up eggplant in salty water:
- Combine 2 teaspoons salt and 1/2 cup water in a cup. Heat in microwave. Stir to ensure salt has dissolved. Pour the salty water into a pot or dish large enough to fit the cut-up eggplant.
- Add cold water to the salty water, enough to cover the eggplant. Stir.
- Add the cut-up eggplant and weigh it down with a water-filled bowl.
- Soak cut-up eggplant for 20 minutes or longer.

Cook the vegetables:
- In a large skillet, cook onions in olive oil on medium heat, about 5 minutes.
- Add eggplant to the skillet. Drizzle on olive oil.
- Add in zucchini, mushrooms, salt and pepper. You may want to add a little water. Cook, covered, until vegetables are done, about 8 minutes.
- Top with shredded cheese.

Serves 2 to 3.

Notes:
*A simpler version: omit onions, mushrooms and/or zucchini, that is, just use eggplant.
*Another idea: omit eggplant; sauté zucchini, mushrooms, and onions in olive oil, salt, and ground black pepper for about 8 minutes.

Skillet Eggplant with Tomatoes

This recipe adds tomatoes to Skillet Eggplant with Zucchini and Mushrooms.

Skillet Eggplant with Zucchini and Mushrooms (see recipe)
Tomatoes, your choice:
> **1 to 2 large fresh tomatoes, quartered**
> **or**
> **1 can (14 oz) stewed tomatoes (either drained or not)**
> **or**
> **1 can (14 oz) whole tomatoes (either drained or not)**

- Follow the recipe for *Skillet Eggplant*. When the vegetables (eggplant, etc.) have cooked 3 to 5 minutes, stir in the tomatoes.
- Cook, covered, on low heat until everything is piping hot, just a few minutes.

Serves 4.

Another idea: omit eggplant; sauté zucchini, mushrooms, and onions in olive oil, salt, and ground black pepper for about 8 minutes. Then add tomatoes and heat.

Cauliflower with Red Bell Pepper

2 Tbsps olive oil (divided)
10 thin strips of sliced red bell pepper*
10 thin strips of sliced onion
1 to 1½ cups thinly sliced cauliflower**
2 Tbsps water
Garlic salt and/or table salt, to taste
Ground black pepper, to taste
To top: bleu cheese crumbles *or*
      shredded cheddar, to top *or*
      ground turmeric, to top

- Pour 1 tablespoon olive oil into a skillet, and add red bell pepper and onion. Sauté for 5 to 8 minutes.
- Add cauliflower, 1 tablespoon oil, 2 tablespoons water, salt, and pepper to the skillet.
- Cover and cook on medium-low, about 10 minutes, occasionally lifting lid to stir.
- Serve and top with cheese or turmeric.

Serves 2.

Notes:
*If you don't have red bell pepper on hand, no worries, cook this dish without it.
**You could use broccoli instead of cauliflower.

Honey Glazed Carrots

1 cup carrots, sliced
1 Tbsp white wine, preferably a sweet wine
Pat of butter
1 tsp olive oil
1 tsp honey
Cinnamon, a couple shakes (optional)
Sage, to taste (optional)

- Steam carrots until they're not quite done, about 3 minutes.
- Transfer the carrots to a saucepan—the bottom saucepan of your steamer set is ideal.
- Add in all of the other ingredients to the saucepan. Cook on medium heat for a few minutes, stirring frequently, until the carrots are done.

Serves 2.

Katy's Kale

*Kale is sold in bunches and in bags. Bunches are comprised of several long stalks and are **much** easier to work with than shredded kale-in-a-bag. Kale's dark green color is shouting, We have lots of nutrients!*

> **4 cups of kale, packed down**
> **2 to 3 Tbsps olive oil (divided)***
> **1 clove garlic**
> **1/3 cup red bell pepper *or* onion, chopped**
> **1/2 to 1 cup water***
> **1 to 2 Tbsps balsamic vinegar***
> **Salt, to taste: garlic, table or seasoned**
> **Ground pepper, to taste: black, cayenne or white**

- Separate the thick stems from the leaves, by tearing the leaves off. Discard the stems. Rinse and drain the leaves in a colander.
- In a skillet, sauté garlic and red bell pepper (or onion) in 1 tablespoon olive oil, about 5 minutes.
- Scoop up the kale up and add it to the skillet.
- Drizzle 1 to 2 tablespoons olive oil over the kale. Cook on medium-low about 3 minutes, tossing the kale frequently.
- Add water and balsamic vinegar to the skillet. Cover and cook on medium-low until tender, about 25 additional minutes.
- Check periodically and add more water and/or oil if desired.

Serves 2.

Notes:
- *The proportion of oil, vinegar, and water will depend on your particular tastes.
- Who is Katy? She is someone special to me that I've known almost my entire life. She likes kale and other vegetables and is especially partial to carrots.

Collard Greens

Before moving to Florida, Steve and I had heard of collard greens but had never eaten them. So when we got here, we bought and cooked them. Honestly, we didn't care for them. But collard greens are an intrinsic part of this region, and we didn't want to give up on them. We tried a few more times and came up with this recipe. And now? We love collards!

> **4 cups (1 quart) collard greens, a big pile!**
> **2 cups water**
> **1/4 to 1/2 cup white wine (sweet or dry, your choice)***
> **3 Tbsps olive oil**
> **1/2 cup onion, chopped**
> **Salt, to taste: garlic, table or seasoned**
> **Ground cayenne, to taste**

- Separate the thick stems from the leaves, by tearing the leaves off. Discard the stems. Rinse and drain the leaves in a colander.
- Into a large skillet, pour the water, wine, and oil. Turn the heat to medium-low.
- Place the collard greens and onions in the skillet.
- Sprinkle in salt and cayenne.
- Cook, covered, on medium-low heat for about 40 minutes. Cook time depends on how tough the leaves are and how hot the stove heat is.
- Every so often, check to ensure the collards aren't sticking to the skillet. Add more water and/or oil, if needed.

Serves 2.

Note: *Sometimes we use 2 tablespoons balsamic vinegar instead of wine.

Curry Vegetables

One or more vegetables, about 2 cups total, cut in bite sizes, such as:

mustard greens	asparagus	zucchini
yellow squash	snow peas	carrots
green beans	bok choy	onion
mushrooms	broccoli	celery
cauliflower	cabbage	peas

1 teaspoon (1 pat) butter
1 tablespoon olive oil
1/2 tsp (or more) curry powder
Soy sauce, as a condiment

- Steam the vegetables until they're not quite done.
- On low heat, in a sauce pan, make a curry sauce by mixing butter, oil, and curry powder.
- Add the veggies to the curry sauce (in the saucepan) and stir. Cook on low heat, stirring frequently, until the veggies are done, just a few minutes.
- Serve with rice. Sprinkle on soy sauce.

Serves 2.

Notes:
- Cabbage and onion go well together. So do cauliflower and peas. Also bok choy and zucchini.
- Serve over or with rice.

This and That

Great Guacamole

I owe my love of guacamole to that nice couple from Morelia, Mexico that I wrote about in Crepes and Coyotes and Other Tales: The Companion Book to Steve and Jannie's Home Cookin' Recipes.

>   **1 avocado, mashed**
>   **1 Tbsp minced onion**
>   **2 tsps lemon or lime juice (Cut into fourths and squeeze a wedge.)**
>   **1 tsp Sriracha sauce (Or green sauce containing tomatillos and omit lemon/lime.)**
>   **Salt, to taste**
>   **Cumin, to taste**
>   **Fresh diced cilantro, to taste**
>   **1 small Roma tomato, diced (optional)**

➢ Combine all ingredients in a mixing bowl *except* tomato.
➢ Now fold in tomato.
➢ Let chill and marinate in the refrigerator *or* just eat it right now.

Serves 2 to 4.

Note: Avocado, citrus, and salt are the three essential ingredients. It's that citrus-salty combo that makes you crave more. If you are lacking some of the other ingredients, simply go with what you've got. ☺

Esteban's Salsa Verde

Steve experimented several times and this is the recipe he likes. Es delicioso.

8 to 10 tomatillos, with paper lanterns and stems removed and cut in quarters
2 cloves garlic, diced
1 serrano pepper, seeded and diced
1/2 red onion or yellow onion, diced
3/4 to 1 cup water
1 Tbsp olive oil
1 tsp cumin
1 tsp chili powder
1 tsp sugar
Salt, to taste
1 bunch cilantro *stems*, chopped
1 bunch cilantro *leaves*, chopped
Juice of 2 limes

➢ Place all ingredients in a large pot, *except* the lime juice and cilantro *leaves*.
➢ Bring to a boil, then lower heat (barely bubbling) and cook until the tomatillos are tender, about 5 minutes.
➢ Put mixture in the refrigerator to cool.
➢ When mixture is no longer hot, put it in a blender and pulse for a few seconds.
➢ Add lime juice and cilantro *leaves* and blend for about 10 more seconds.
➢ Refrigerate.

Salsa Verde ideas:
- on tacos, quesadillas, and chips
- in chopped cabbage, as a coleslaw (This is delicious!)
- poured over baked or sautéed chicken
- poured over enchiladas and then baked

Quesadillas and Soft Tacos

If you are lacking some of the ingredients, simply go with what you've got.

Quesadilla   or   **Soft Taco**
1 flour tortilla   2 corn tortillas

Build your quesadilla or soft taco with these ingredients:
Already-cooked chicken*, pork, beef, or shrimp, cut into bite sizes
Cheese, shredded
Tomatoes, diced (raw or sautéed)
Onion, diced (raw or sautéed)
Olives, chopped
Cumin
Sriracha (or any kind of hot sauce that you like)

Toppings:
Guacamole (see recipe) or chopped avocado
Cilantro
Sour cream or plain yogurt
Salsa, such as *Esteban's Salsa Verde* (see recipe)

- Place the tortilla(s) on a plate or paper towel.
- Pile all of your ingredients on the tortilla(s) *except* the toppings.
- Fold your quesadilla or taco in half (optional).
- Heat in the microwave for about 40 seconds.
- Add your toppings.

Serves 1.

Note: *You can use chicken from leftover *Chicken-in-a-Pot*.

Pigs in a Serape

One day at lunch Steve wanted hotdogs. We didn't have any buns but we did have flour tortillas. So, we wrapped the hotdogs in tortillas. It works!

One flour tortilla*
One hotdog
Cheese, grated or cubed
Onion, minced
Mustard or Sriracha sauce

➢ Place the tortilla on a plate or paper towel.
➢ Place the hotdog on the tortilla.
➢ Put cheese, onion, and mustard (or Sriracha) on the tortilla.
➢ Roll the "serape."
➢ Heat in the microwave for about 30 seconds.

Serves 1.

Notes:
- *If tortilla is super-large size, you can use one-half tortilla per hotdog.
- You can smother this with canned chili and beans.

Thai Pizza

Sweet Chili Sauce—that pinkish-red, syrupy Thai concoction—might seem strange to put on pizza, but you are in for a pleasant surprise. Leftover chicken is a natural for this dish. No quantities given because that depends on the size of your pizza and your personal taste.

Premium frozen cheese pizza
Chicken, already cooked, chopped*
Mushrooms, chopped
Olive oil (to sauté veggies)
Broccoli, chopped
Onion, chopped
Thai sweet chili sauce

➢ In a skillet, sauté the mushrooms in a little olive oil.
➢ As the mushrooms begin to release their juices, add the broccoli and onion. Add a tablespoon of water, if needed. Cook until the mushroom juices evaporate.
➢ Arrange the chicken and veggies on the pizza.
➢ Pour sweet chili sauce on the pizza.
➢ Bake pizza according to directions on the package.

Note: *You can use chicken from leftover *Chicken-in-a-Pot*.

Sautéed Shrimp over Rice

*When using already-cooked shrimp, just **heat** them, don't cook them. Otherwise, they will turn tough, and you won't want to eat them, and you may cry tears of humiliation like I did years ago, although I should have laughed—I would have felt better, as would everyone else!*

10 to 12 extra-large frozen cooked shrimp, deveined
2/3 cup brown rice
2 Tbsps olive oil (divided)
1/2 cup chopped onions
1 to 1½ cups chopped mushrooms
Salt, to taste: garlic, table, or seasoned

- Defrost already-cooked shrimp according to directions on package.
- Start cooking rice according to directions on package.
- In a skillet, sauté onions in a tablespoon of olive oil. Set aside in a small dish.
- In same skillet, sauté mushrooms in a tablespoon of olive oil, about 3 minutes.
- Add shrimp to the mushroom skillet, and add back in the onions.
- Heat on medium-low, covered, for just a few minutes. (Don't overcook those shrimp!)
- Serve over rice.

Serves 2.

Notes:
- You can add in hot pepper sauce or soy sauce.
- If you have leftover rice, consider baking *Apple Raisin Rice Custard* (see recipe in Desserts section).

Joey's Marinara Sauce

Joey cooked a larger quantity than this recipe, but the proportions are right. (Stories about Joey are in Crepes and Coyotes and Other Tales.*) You can add in cooked meat—see recipes for* Seasoned Ground Beef, Swedish Meatballs, *and* Our Down-home Meatloaf *in the Beef section—but it's also great like this, as a vegetarian sauce. Serve over pasta, such as spaghetti or ravioli.*

1 clove garlic, minced
1/4 cup olive oil (divided)
1/2 onion, chopped
8 mushrooms, chopped (optional)
One 6 oz can tomato paste
One 8 oz *or* 16 oz can tomato sauce (your call)
One 15 can whole tomatoes or diced tomatoes

1/2 cup red wine
3/4 tsp thyme
3/4 tsp oregano
1/2 tsp black pepper

- In a large soup pot, sauté garlic and onions in 2 tablespoons of olive oil on medium heat, about 7 minutes.
- Add in mushrooms, a tablespoon of olive oil, and sauté about 5 minutes.
- Stir in a can of tomato paste.
- Stir in a can of tomato sauce.
- Stir in a can of whole (or diced) tomatoes.
- Pour red wine into a wine glass and drink it. Stir—the pot, that is.
- Stir in red wine, a tablespoon of olive oil, and spices.
- Simmer, covered, for 90 minutes or longer. Stir occasionally.

Serves 4.

Suggestion: Pour this sauce over *Stefano's Easy Chicken Cacciatore.*

Spaghetti Stretcher

This dish is simply "spaghetti sauce" with kidney beans. It's a good way to use up leftover red sauce. By adding in the beans you stretch your inventory, making it go farther.

Pasta, such as spaghetti
Canned kidney beans, about 1/4 cup per serving
Italian red sauce with or without ground beef, such as:
    Joey's Marinara **with *Seasoned Ground Beef*****
    or **your own spaghetti sauce**
    or **spaghetti sauce in a jar**

- Cook the pasta according to directions on the package.
- In a separate sauce pan, mix Italian red sauce with canned kidney beans.
- Thoroughly heat this mixture, stirring, letting it gently bubble for a few minutes.
- Serve over pasta.

Notes:
**Joey's Marinara* recipe is the previous one.
***Seasoned Ground Beef* recipe is in the Beef section.

Vegetables in Mild Marinara Sauce

This is Turkey Spaghetti *without the ground turkey. You can create many variations, depending on the vegetables you choose.*

    1 cup chopped onion
    1 tablespoon olive oil
    1/4 tsp oregano
    1/4 tsp thyme
    Ground black pepper to taste
    2 Tbsps diced marinated sun-dried tomatoes
    2 Tbsps oil from sun-dried tomatoes jar (or use olive oil)
    1 cup chopped mushrooms
    1/2 to 1 cup shredded carrot
    1½ cups of chopped vegetables, such as:
        cauliflower   zucchini   broccoli   celery
        bell pepper   eggplant   chard   corn
    1 cup beef broth
    1 can (14 oz) crushed tomatoes (Or 28 oz can for more tomato flavor)
    2 Tbsps cornstarch and 2 Tbsps cold water
    Pasta, such as angel hair

- In a large skillet, sauté onions in olive oil, 5 to 7 minutes.
- Add in seasonings, sun-dried tomato and its oil, mushrooms, carrot, and other vegetables. Cook on low, covered, about 5 minutes.
- Separately cook pasta using the directions on the package. Set aside.
- Stir in beef broth and crushed tomatoes. Simmer 5 to 10 minutes.
- Thicken the sauce: In a cup, mix 2 tablespoons each of cornstarch and cold water. Spoon into the bubbling sauce. May not need all of it.

Serves 3 or 4.

Darla's Pasta Primavera

Darla is a first grade teacher. She cooked dinner for a few of us teachers one evening at her home, and the next day, after school, I stopped by her classroom and asked for the recipe, jotting it down on paper that was handy—that brown, wide-ruled first- grade paper. Still have that piece of paper in a recipe binder. I've added a chicken and shrimp option.

1 cup bowtie pasta (uncooked) **Dried oregano, dash**
1 clove of garlic **2 Tbsps sun-dried tomatoes, chopped**
1/4 cup olive oil (divided) **8 Kalamata olives, halved**
1/2 cup onion, chopped **1/4 cup red wine**
1 cup mushrooms, chopped **1 cup spinach, chopped***
1 cup broccoli, cut up **Salt, to taste**
1/2 cup asparagus, cut up **Ground black pepper, to taste**
  Shredded parmesan, to top
**Optional: already-cooked chicken, e.g., leftover *Chicken-in-a-Pot*
or already-cooked shrimp in the amount you like**

- Cook bowtie pasta using the directions on the package. Drain. Set aside.
- In a large skillet, sauté garlic in 1 tablespoon olive oil, about 3 minutes.
- Add in chopped onions and 1 tablespoon olive oil. Sauté about 3 minutes.
- Add in mushrooms, broccoli, asparagus, dash of oregano, sun-dried tomatoes, olives, red wine, *already-cooked* chicken or shrimp, and remaining olive oil. Cook, covered, on low heat, about 3 minutes.
- Add in spinach and bowties. Cook, covered, on low heat, about 3 minutes.
- Serve and top with parmesan.

Serves 2.

Note: *Instead of spinach you can use kale, beet greens, mustard greens, or the green part of bok choy.

Steve's Three-Cheese Lasagna

1/2 lb *Seasoned Ground Beef* (see recipe in Beef section)
2 cups Italian red sauce: from a jar *or*
   ***Joey's Marinara* (see recipe in This and That section)**
8 oz lasagna noodles (half of a 1 lb package)
1/2 cup sliced ripe olives
1/2 cup grated parmesan
1/2 cup shredded mozzarella
1/2 cup ricotta cheese
Nonstick cooking oil spray

- Set aside your *Seasoned Ground Beef*.
- Boil lasagna according to directions on the package.
- Spray nonstick cooking oil into an 8 x 11 inch baking dish.
- Arrange a layer of lasagna noodles in the baking dish. (You may want to cut some of them so they fit better.)
- Layer the other ingredients on top of the pasta in this order:
    - *Seasoned Ground Beef*
    - Italian red sauce
    - Olives
    - The three cheeses
- Make a second layer, just like the first one.
- Lay down a third layer of lasagna noodles and put cheese on top of this one.
- Cover baking dish with aluminum foil.
- Bake at 350 degrees for about 45 minutes.
- When serving, cut rectangular-shaped pieces with a knife and lift each piece out with a spatula.

Serves 4.

Paula's Party Dip

"They're gonna love it," our friend Paula reassured Chris and me when she told us the recipe to this dip back in the early 1980s. The partygoers, it turned out, couldn't get enough of that dip. In fact, we ran out pretty early on.

1 part Ricotta, low fat
1 part Cottage cheese, low fat
1 part Neufchatel Cheese
Fresh minced parsley, as much as you like
Dill, to taste
Salt, to taste
Ground black pepper or cayenne, to taste
Ground cayenne pepper, to taste

➢ Fold all of the ingredients together in a large mixing bowl. Careful not to mix too vigorously or else the cheeses will soften and the dip will be too soft.
➢ Serve with Vegetable Thin Crackers.

Note: An alternative is to use just 2 of the 3 cheeses.

S & J's Deviled Eggs

Use the amounts and proportions that are right for you.

Hard boiled eggs
Mayonnaise
Pickle relish
Mustard
Capers
Sriracha hot chili sauce
Paprika, to top

- Peel the eggs and cut each one in half, lengthwise.
- Scoop the yolks out into a bowl and mash them. Set the white parts aside.
- Put all of the condiments into the bowl of mashed egg yolks. Mix thoroughly.
- Using two spoons, put a spoonful of the mixture into the hollow of each egg white.
- Chill in the refrigerator.

Note: With 5 eggs, I use *about* a tablespoon *each* of mayo, mustard, pickle relish, and capers; 1/2 teaspoon of Sriracha.

The Veggieloaf

Veggieloaf is similar to meatloaf, but instead of ground beef, you use brown rice, cheese, and vegetables. It's a nifty vegetarian alternative.

This dish is limited only by your imagination. For instance, you could take the recipe for *Broccoli and Mushroom Veggieloaf* and make any or all of these changes:

- You could use other vegetables, such as eggplant, broccoli, tomatoes, chard, spinach, and/or kale.
- You could use sun-dried tomatoes or green bell pepper or jalapeno instead of red bell pepper.
- You could omit some of the vegetables.
- You could change their relative amounts.
- You could use different cheeses.

A few more points:

- If you're cooking for one or two, you're going to have some Veggieloaf left over. This is a good thing; it means *inventory* ☺. You don't have to bake tomorrow—just heat and eat.

- A word about *rice*. Steve suggests you cook more rice than the recipe calls for, say, twice the rice needed for the Veggieloaf. By saving half for something else, you have one less thing to do when you cook tomorrow. More inventory.

- Experiment! Have fun and be creative. Mad cook in the kitchen!

Broccoli and Mushroom Veggieloaf

A complete vegetarian meal. Lots of ingredients, but it's easy to make.

- 2/3 cup uncooked brown rice
- 1/4 tsp salt
- 1 to 2 Tbsps olive oil (divided)
- 1 clove garlic, minced
- 1/2 cup chopped onion
- 3 Tbsps diced fresh red bell pepper *or* marinated piemento (jar or can)
- 1½ cups chopped mushrooms
- 1 cup diced broccoli florets
- 1 cup shredded carrot
- 3/4 cup shredded zucchini
- 1/2 cup diced fresh parsley
- 1/2 cup shredded Jack cheese
- 1/2 cup shredded cheddar
- 3 eggs, lightly beaten
- Ground cayenne, to taste
- Nonstick cooking oil spray

➢ Cook the brown rice along with some salt. Set aside.
➢ Meanwhile, pour olive oil in a skillet. Sauté garlic, onions and red bell pepper. (If you're using marinated piemento, no need to sauté it.) When they're done, spoon them into a large mixing bowl.
➢ Sauté mushrooms in olive oil, then add them to the large bowl.
➢ Add the raw vegetables to the large bowl: broccoli, carrot, zucchini and parsley. Mix thoroughly.
➢ Add in the cheeses, eggs, and cayenne. Mix thoroughly.
➢ Oil an 8 x 8 inch baking dish with nonstick cooking oil spray.*
➢ Spoon the mixture into your baking dish.
➢ Bake at 350 degrees for about 45 minutes.

Serves 4 to 6.

Note: *I call this dish "Veggie*loaf*" and yet, like Meatloaf, I bake it in a baking dish, not a meatloaf pan. I do this is to reduce the baking time.

Chicken Salad Sandwiches

Two options: fresh chicken or canned chicken.

Use:

    **1½ cups chopped, fresh, already-cooked chicken,
such as leftover *Chicken-in-a-Pot***
    2 Tbsps mayonnaise

or

    1 can (12 oz) chicken
    1 Tbsp mayonnaise (optional)

For both recipes:

    1 Tbsp minced pimiento *or* red bell pepper
    ***or* 2 Tbsps green olives stuffed with pimiento**
    2 Tbsps capers
    1 tsp caper juice
    Ground pepper, to taste: black or white
    3 or 4 whole grain bread slices
    Cucumber slices and/or tomato slices

- Mix ingredients in a bowl (*except* bread, cucumber, and tomato).
- Spoon the chicken salad onto the bread.
- Add cucumber and/or tomato slices.

Serves 2.

Notes:
- I keep canned chicken as emergency food. As time passes and I have no emergencies, I bring it out and make chicken salad.
- You can use the *Tuna Salad* recipe instead or some hybrid of the two.

Curry Chicken Salad Sandwiches

1/4 cup plain yogurt
2 tsps curry powder
1/2 tsp sugar
1½ cups cold cooked chicken, chopped*
1/4 cup broccoli, diced
2 Tbsps celery, diced
1 Tbsp onion, minced
2 Tbsps raisins
1 Tbsp sunflower seeds
Salt, to taste

3 or 4 whole grain bread slices

- Mix yogurt, curry powder, and sugar in a medium bowl until well blended.
- Mix in chicken, broccoli, celery, and onion.
- Add in raisins and sunflower seeds.
- Taste and, if you want salt added, do so now.
- Spoon the chicken salad onto your bread.

Serves 2.

Note: *You can use chicken from leftover *Chicken-in-a-Pot*.

Tuna Salad Sandwiches

The citrus juice gives this tuna salad some zip.

	5 oz net weight	**7 oz net weight**
1 can of tuna*	4 oz drain wt	5.4 oz drain wt
Celery *or* cucumber, diced	2 Tbsps	3 Tbsps
Olives, any kind, chopped	6	8
Mayonnaise	1½ Tbsps	2 Tbsps
Lemon or lime juice	1½ Tbsps	2 Tbsps
Pickle relish	1½ Tbsps	2 Tbsps
Onion, minced (optional)	2 tsps	1 Tbsp

3 or 4 whole grain bread slices
Tomato slices

- Mix ingredients in a bowl (*except* the bread and tomato slices).
- Spoon the tuna salad onto your bread.
- Add tomato slices.

Serves 2.

Notes:
- *I use solid white albacore.
- If you don't have all of these ingredients, go with what you do have.

Fried Tofu

*Tofu has no taste and that's the beauty of it—**you** add the flavor. In this recipe the flavor comes from sesame seed oil and soy sauce. So simple, so good; it's a nice side dish for your Asian meal.*

> **4 slices tofu**
> **2 Tbsps soy sauce**
> **2 tsps vegetable oil**
> **1 tsp sesame seed oil**
> **Nonstick cooking oil spray**

➢ <u>Prepare the tofu</u>:
- Pour 1 Tbsp soy sauce onto a dinner plate.
- Slice the tofu in its package, about 1/2 inch thick slices.
- Carefully place each slice on the soy sauce plate.
- Pour 1 more tablespoon soy sauce on the top of each slice.

➢ <u>Fry the tofu</u>:
- Heat a skillet on medium-high.
- Pour vegetable oil and sesame seed oil onto the skillet and swirl it around.
- Spray nonstick cooking oil onto the skillet.
- Place tofu slices into the skillet.
- Cook the tofu slices fast for a few minutes.
- Flip each slice and fry a couple more minutes.
- Serve piping hot.

Serves 2.

Note: Fried Tofu is best piping hot. If it sits for more than a couple of minutes, put it on a plate, cover with a paper towel, and heat it in your microwave for a few seconds.

Desserts

Raisin Cornmeal Custard

2 Tbsps cornmeal*
1/3 cup raisins
1 tsp sugar
4 eggs
3 Tbsps honey
1½ tsps vanilla
2 cups milk
Ground nutmeg, to taste

Nonstick cooking oil spray
Six 1-cup Pyrex cups
Cookie sheet

- Lightly spray the bottom of 6 Pyrex cups with nonstick cooking oil.
- Measure out cornmeal and raisins and keep them separate, e.g., keep each in a small bowl.
- Mix together sugar and cornmeal.
- Spoon the sweetened cornmeal, and then the raisins, into 6 small Pyrex cups, evenly dividing these two.
- In a large bowl, whisk eggs, honey, and vanilla.
- Add in milk and whisk.
- Spoon or pour the milk mixture into each cup
- Sprinkle nutmeg on the top of each filled cup.
- Place each cup on a cookie sheet.
- Bake at 350 degrees for about 35 minutes.

Serves 6.

Note: *The cornmeal sits at the bottom and forms a thin crust. The whey (liquid) is absorbed into the cornmeal.

Apple Raisin Rice Custard

1/2 cup already-cooked white or brown rice*
1/2 cup apple, shredded or diced—any kind**
1/3 cup golden raisins (or regular raisins)
1 tsp sugar
3 eggs
1 Tbsp honey   **Nonstick cooking oil spray**
1 tsp vanilla extract (optional)   **Five 1-cup Pyrex cups**
1½ cups milk   **Cookie sheet**
Ground allspice, to taste

- Measure out rice, apple, and raisins into their own small bowl—keeping each of these three ingredients separate.
- Sprinkle sugar over the rice and mix.
- Spoon the sweetened rice, apple, and raisins into 5 small Pyrex cups—in that order—evenly dividing these three.
- In a large bowl, whisk eggs, honey, and vanilla.
- Add in milk and whisk.
- Spoon or pour the milk mixture into each cup.
- Sprinkle allspice on the tops of each filled cup.
- Place cups on a cookie sheet.
- Bake at 350 degrees for about 35 minutes.

Serves 5.

Notes:
*The rice sits at the bottom. The whey (liquid) is absorbed into the rice.
**Half of a fresh pear is also very good instead of fresh apple.

Creamy Lemon Pie
(Tofu Yogurt Lemon Pie)

Tofu in a pie? Yes, and yogurt, too! Sounds weird but it's rich and lemony and satisfying and has a cheesecake-like texture.

3 Tbsps cornstarch	**1 Tbsp sugar**
3 Tbsps cold water	**3 Tbsps oil**
3/4 lb (12 oz) silken tofu*	**1/4 cup honey**
1 cup plain yogurt	**2 tsps vanilla**
1/4 cup lemon juice	**Graham cracker pie crust**

- In a cup, combine 3 tablespoons cornstarch with 3 tablespoons water. Stir until cornstarch dissolves. Set aside.
- Put all ingredients (*except* the pie crust) into a blender, with the cornstarch water going in last.
- Blend until smooth—*only a few seconds* (or else the filling will be too runny).
- Pour filling into the graham cracker pie crust.
- Bake at 350 degrees for 45 to 50 minutes, until the edge of the filling starts to brown and the middle barely wiggles.
- Let cool before cutting slices.

Serves 6 to 8.

Notes:
*Use SILKEN tofu to achieve the right consistency—firm tofu will not work!!
*Use three-fourths of a one-pound package.

New Fairy Cookies

Slightly chewy, definitely peanut buttery…they are hippie cookies.

For 24 small cookies	For 12 small cookies
Dry ingredients:	**Dry ingredients:**
1/2 cup whole wheat flour	**1/4 cup whole wheat flour**
1/4 cup wheat germ	**2 Tbsps wheat germ**
2 Tbsps rolled oats	**1 Tbsp old-fashioned oats**
2 Tbsps sunflower seeds	**1 Tbsp sunflower seeds**
1 tsp baking powder	**1/2 tsp baking powder**
1/8 tsp salt	**few pinches of salt**
2/3 cup raisins and/or other dried fruit	**1/3 cup raisins, etc.**
2/3 cup sugar*	**1/3 cup sugar***
Wet ingredients:	**Wet ingredients:**
2 eggs	**1 egg**
1/4 cup vegetable oil	**2 Tbsps vegetable oil**
1 tsp vanilla extract	**1/2 tsp vanilla extract**
2/3 cup peanut butter	**1/3 cup peanut butter**
1/3 cup bittersweet choc baking chips	**3 Tbsps bittersweet chocolate chips**

Non-stick cooking oil spray for the cookie sheet

- Mix the dry ingredients in a bowl.
- Mix the wet ingredients in another bowl.
- Pour the dry into the wet and stir.
- Spray nonstick cooking oil onto baking sheet.
- Form batter into lumps (I use 2 spoons) and place on baking sheet.
- Push chocolate chips into each cookie.
- Bake at 350 degrees for about 15 minutes.

Note: *You can use less sugar: 1/2 cup for the 24-cookie recipe and 1/4 cup for the 12-cookie recipe.

Cocoa Cake

Vinegar in a cake? Don't worry, you won't taste any vinegar. This is a culinary science project: the vinegar and baking soda react with each other to create a light, moist cake. Low in sugar compared to most cake recipes. No egg needed. Easy to make!

Dry ingredients:
1¼ cup whole wheat flour
1/4 cup unbleached white flour
2/3 cup sugar
1/4 cup cocoa*
1¼ tsp baking soda
1/2 tsp salt

Wet ingredients:
1 Tbsp vinegar
1 Tbsp + 1 tsp vanilla extract
1/2 cup vegetable oil
1 cup very warm water

Confectioner's sugar (powdered sugar) to dust the top

- Mix the dry ingredients in a medium bowl.
- Mix the wet ingredients in a large bowl.
- Pour the dry into the wet and stir.
- Pour the batter into an 8 x 8 inch baking dish.
- Bake at 350 degrees for 25 minutes.
- Let cool before cutting slices (or else cake will break apart).
- Dust top with powdered sugar.

Serves 6 to 10, depending on how much cake everyone wants.

Notes:
- *By "cocoa" I mean unsweetened, 100% pure cocoa. It's in powder form and found in your grocery store's baking aisle.
- This recipe is flexible: You can use 1/2 cup sugar and 1/4 cup oil. Also, you can add in an egg; if you do, use 7/8 cup (7 oz) very warm water instead of 1 cup.

Pear and Apple Crisp

Good any time of day or night—even breakfast!

3 cups fruit:
    2 Bartlett pears, cubed*
    1 apple, cubed*
3 Tbsps old-fashioned oats or quick oats
3 Tbsps unbleached white flour
1½ Tbsps sugar
1 Tbsp canola oil
1 Tbsp soft butter
3 Tbsps hot water
1/2 tsp ground cinnamon

- Measure out the fruit. Set aside.
- In a small bowl, mix together oats, flour, and sugar.
- In another small bowl mix together oil and soft butter.
- Combine dry with wet and mix until well blended. Set aside.
- Pour 3 tablespoons hot water into an 8 x 8 inch baking dish.
- Arrange the fruit on top of the water, then sprinkle on the cinnamon.
- Using two spoons, put tiny globs of the sugar-flour mixture on top of the fruit. (If it doesn't quite glob, mix in a little more oil.)
- Bake at 400 degrees for about 30 minutes.

Serves 3.

Notes:
*We've used a variety of apples, and they're all good: Gala, Jazz, McIntosh, Opal, Granny Smith, and combinations.
*You can use apples-only. And you can use Bartlett pears-only. Doesn't have to be both.

Pear and Blackberry Crisp

This recipe is exactly like Pear and Apple Crisp *except that it's smaller and uses another combination of fruit. You might like to experiment with other combos, too.*

2 cups fruit:
    1 Bartlett pear, cubed
    1 cup blackberries
2 Tbsps old-fashioned oats or quick oats
2 Tbsps unbleached white flour
1 Tbsp sugar
2 tsps canola oil
2 tsps soft butter
2 Tbsps hot water
1/4 tsp ground cinnamon

- Measure out the fruit. Set aside.
- In a small bowl, mix together oats, flour, and sugar.
- In another small bowl mix together oil and soft butter.
- Combine dry with wet and mix until well blended. Set aside.
- Pour 2 tablespoons hot water into a 6 x 6 inch baking dish. (Could be smaller.)
- Arrange the fruit on top of the water, then sprinkle on the cinnamon.
- Using two spoons, put tiny globs of the sugar-flour mixture on top of the fruit. (If it doesn't quite glob, mix in a little more oil.)
- Bake at 400 degrees for about 30 minutes.

Serves 2.

Anytime Skillet Apples

For dessert, late night snack, breakfast—anytime, actually!

1 apple
1 pat of butter
Ground cinnamon, to taste
Honey, to taste

- Slice apple very thinly.
- Heat a skillet on medium and melt a pat of butter.
- Place apple slices in skillet.
- Sprinkle cinnamon over the apple slices.
- Drizzle on some honey.
- After a couple minutes or so, flip apples onto their other side.
- Let them quietly cook for another minute or so.

Serves 2.

Quick Bread

A Grand Variety of Quick Breads

Quick bread can be made in an infinite number of ways! You can start with *Jannie's Basic Quick Bread* and change something. For example:

- Omit cornmeal.
- Use a different ratio of white flour to whole wheat.
- Use non-wheat flours or combine them with whole wheat flour.
- Use wheat germ.
- Use wheat bran.
- Use a combo of sweeteners—sugar, honey, brown sugar—or just one.
- Use peanut oil instead of canola oil.
- Add 1/2 mashed banana. (Use less sweetener and milk.)
- Add diced fresh apple.
- Add dried fruit: apple, apricots, cranberries, currants, figs, golden raisins, and/or regular raisins.
- Add nuts and seeds.
- Use fresh or frozen fruit. (Use less milk.)
- Use plain yogurt. (Use more sweetener.)
- Use plain yogurt *and* milk. (Use more sweetener.)
- Omit the vanilla extract.

A couple things I've learned:

- You may want to store flour in the freezer or refrigerator. Keeps the bugs out. Just saying.

- Humidity plays a big role in baking. On rainy mornings, I need less liquid and more bake time. I tested all of these recipes in Florida—a pretty humid place. You may need to adjust bake time and the amount of liquid, baking powder, and baking soda.

More Quick Bread Comments

- If you're baking for yourself, you're going to have some quick bread left over. This is a good thing. It means *inventory*. ☺ It means you don't have to bake tomorrow—just eat. Less baking time, more eating time.

- I hesitate to specify the amount of spices—cinnamon, nutmeg, and allspice—because (as I've mentioned before): 1) people's palates and preferences differ and 2) the strength of a spice changes over time. I prefer a lot of spice, not only because it tastes good, but also because I need less sweetener when I spice it up.

- About sugar and oil: I use a minimal amount. You may prefer to add more.

- A shortcut to measuring 3 tablespoons is to fill a 1/4 measuring cup three-quarters full (although when I tested these recipes, I filled a tablespoon 3 times).

- *Jannie's Basic Quick Bread* is the first recipe in this section; the ones that follow merely add and omit a few ingredients. I hope you experiment and create your own quick bread recipes. It's fun!

Jannie's Basic Quick Bread

This is my basic quick bread recipe, my starting place.
The other recipes are variations on this theme, as I add and omit ingredients.

Dry ingredients	**Wet ingredients**
3/4 cup whole wheat flour	1 egg
1/4 cup unbleached white flour*	3 Tbsps canola oil
2 Tbsps cornmeal**	2 Tbsps honey
1 Tbsp sugar (optional)	1 tsp vanilla extract
1/2 tsp + 1/8 tsp baking powder	2/3 cup milk
1/2 tsp baking soda	
1/4 tsp salt	

Nonstick cooking oil spray

- Mix the dry ingredients in a medium bowl.
- In a large bowl, whisk the egg.
- Add the other wet ingredients to the beaten egg and whisk.
- Pour the dry ingredients into the wet ingredients. Stir lightly, scraping the spoon along the edge of the bowl.
- Oil an 8 x 8 inch baking dish with nonstick cooking oil spray.
- Pour in the batter. Scrape the bowl clean with a rubber spatula.
- Bake at 350 degrees, 18 to 20 minutes.

Serves 3 or 4.

Notes:
*I love the taste of whole wheat, but a little white flour gives a lighter texture.
**That little bit of cornmeal gives a subtle crunchiness.

It's a Meditation

Early morning in my kitchen and—having decided which quick bread recipe to use—I get down to it. First, a medium bowl for the dry ingredients, then a spoon and knife. I gather measuring spoons and cups together. Next, I open the freezer and lift the flours out, setting them onto the counter. I start measuring, shoveling flour over the top of the cup and leveling it off with the back of a knife.

And so begins my meditation, imperfect as it always is.

These calm motions, these familiar movements, put me in a good frame of mind. I inhale slowly and deeply, taking my time; there's no hurry. I hear my Tai Chi teacher's voice in my head telling us to bend our knees slightly, drop our shoulders, and relax our lower backs. More measuring, more deep breaths. It's almost blissful knowing I'm doing exactly what I want to be doing at this moment—creating this quick bread in my quiet kitchen.

Hippie Quick Bread

No white flour or white sugar in this recipe! Reminds me of my funny-strange two-month stint in the Pacific Northwest. (See "Fairy Cookies in Oregon" and "The Vegetarian" in Crepes and Coyotes and Other Tales*). This was where I learned to bake with whole wheat flour and honey. Changed my life!*

Dry ingredients	**Wet ingredients**
3/4 cup whole wheat flour	1 egg
2 Tbsps wheat bran	3 Tbsps canola oil
2 Tbsps wheat germ	2 Tbsps honey (or more)
1/2 tsp + 1/8 tsp baking powder	1 tsp vanilla extract
1/2 tsp baking soda	2/3 cup milk
1/4 tsp salt	2/3 cup dried fruit*
2 Tbsps sunflower seeds	

Nonstick cooking oil

- Mix the dry ingredients in a medium bowl.
- In a large bowl, whisk the egg.
- Add the other wet ingredients to the beaten egg and whisk.
- Pour the dry ingredients into the wet ingredients. Stir lightly, scraping the spoon along the edge of the bowl.
- Oil an 8 x 8 inch baking dish with nonstick cooking oil spray.
- Pour in the batter. Scrape the bowl clean with a rubber spatula.
- Bake at 350 degrees, about 20 minutes.

Serves 4.

Note: *Dried fruit could be golden raisins, regular raisins, apples, apricots, cranberries, currants, and/or figs. In the 1970s, I used currants.

Cinnamon Apple Raisin Quick Bread

Dry ingredients	**Wet ingredients**
3/4 cup whole wheat flour	1 egg
1/4 cup unbleached white flour	3 Tbsps canola oil
1 Tbsp sugar (optional)	2 Tbsps honey
1¼ tsp cinnamon	1 tsp vanilla extract
1/2 tsp + 1/8 tsp baking powder	1/2 cup milk
1/2 tsp baking soda	3/4 cup apple, diced (1 small)*
1/4 tsp salt	1/2 cup raisins*

Nonstick cooking oil spray

- Mix the dry ingredients in a medium bowl.
- In a large bowl, whisk the egg.
- Add the other wet ingredients to the beaten egg and whisk.
- Pour the dry ingredients into the wet ingredients. Stir lightly, scraping the spoon along the edge of the bowl.
- Oil an 8 x 8 inch baking dish with nonstick cooking oil spray.
- Pour in the batter. Scrape the bowl clean with a rubber spatula.
- Bake at 350 degrees, 20 to 25 minutes.

Serves 4.

Notes: *As for fruit, this recipe is very flexible. You could use:
- pear instead of apple.
- apple only or raisins only.
- dried apricots, cranberries, and/or figs—with or instead of raisins.

Orange Juice Apple Quick Bread

Dry ingredients
3/4 cup whole wheat flour
1/4 cup unbleached white flour
1¼ tsp cinnamon
1/2 tsp + 1/8 tsp baking powder
1/2 tsp baking soda
1/4 tsp salt

Wet ingredients
1 egg
1/3 cup frozen orange juice conc.
1/4 cup canola oil
2 Tbsps honey
1 tsp vanilla extract
1/4 cup milk
1 cup apple, diced (1 small)*

Nonstick cooking oil spray

- Mix the dry ingredients in a medium bowl.
- In a large bowl, whisk the egg.
- Add the other wet ingredients to the beaten egg and whisk.
- Pour the dry ingredients into the wet ingredients. Stir lightly, scraping the spoon along the edge of the bowl.
- Oil an 8 x 8 inch baking dish with nonstick cooking oil spray.
- Pour in the batter. Scrape the bowl clean with a rubber spatula.
- Bake at 350 degrees, 20 to 25 minutes.

Serves 4.

Note: *Pear can be used instead of apple.

Nutmeg Fruit Quick Bread

Dry ingredients
2/3 cup whole wheat flour
1/4 cup unbleached white flour
1/4 cup wheat germ*
2 Tbsps old-fashioned oats*
2 Tbsps chopped almonds
1/4 to 1/2 tsp nutmeg**
1/2 tsp + 1/8 tsp baking powder
1/2 tsp baking soda
1/4 tsp salt

Wet ingredients
1 egg
3 Tbsps canola oil
2 to 3 Tbsps honey
1 tsp vanilla extract
3/4 cup milk
1/2 to 2/3 cup dried fruit combo: apricots, figs, cranberries, raisins

Nonstick cooking oil spray

- Mix the dry ingredients in a medium bowl.
- In a large bowl, whisk the egg.
- Add the other wet ingredients to the beaten egg and whisk.
- Pour the dry ingredients into the wet ingredients. Stir lightly, scraping the spoon along the edge of the bowl.
- Oil an 8 x 8 inch baking dish with nonstick cooking oil spray.
- Pour in the batter. Scrape the bowl clean with a rubber spatula.
- Bake at 350 degrees, 20 to 25 minutes.

Serves 4.

Notes:
*Also good without wheat germ and oats, but adjust recipe as follows: Use an additional 1 to 2 tablespoons whole wheat flour.
**You can use 1 teaspoon allspice instead of nutmeg, or a combination of both.

Exuberance Quick Bread

You're in a good mood—happy to have another day on Earth—and you want to express yourself by throwing everything in. **That's** *when you use this recipe.*

Dry ingredients	**Wet ingredients**
1/2 cup whole wheat flour	1/4 cup mashed banana (1/2 banana)
1/4 cup unbleached white flour	1 egg
2 Tbsps buckwheat flour	3 Tbsps canola oil
1 Tbsp wheat germ	2 Tbsps honey
1 Tbsp cornmeal	1 tsp vanilla extract
2 Tbsps sunflower seeds	2/3 cup milk
1/2 tsp + 1/8 tsp baking powder	1/4 cup chopped dried apricots (6)
1/2 tsp baking soda	1/4 cup raisins
1/4 tsp salt	3 Tbsps dried cranberries
1/2 tsp allspice	
1/2 tsp cinnamon	
1/4 tsp clove	**Nonstick cooking oil spray**

- Mix the dry ingredients in a medium bowl.
- In a large bowl, whisk the egg.
- Add the other wet ingredients to the beaten egg and whisk.
- Pour the dry ingredients into the wet ingredients. Stir lightly, scraping the spoon along the edge of the bowl.
- Oil an 8 x 8 inch baking dish with nonstick cooking oil spray.
- Pour in the batter. Scrape the bowl clean with a rubber spatula.
- Bake at 350 degrees, 20 to 25 minutes.

Serves 4.

Honey Bran Raisin Muffins

Bran muffins remind me of early mornings long ago in San Francisco's Financial District. Most mornings I ate breakfast at home, but there were times when I rolled out of bed and got myself downtown, then grabbed a bran muffin at a takeout bakery before my workday started.

Dry ingredients	Wet ingredients
1/2 cup wheat bran*	1 egg
1/2 cup whole wheat flour	3 Tbsps to 1/4 cup canola oil
1/2 tsp + 1/8 tsp baking powder	2 Tbsps honey
1/2 tsp baking soda	1 tsp vanilla extract
2 Tbsps sugar	1/2 cup milk
1/4 tsp salt	2/3 cup raisins
1/2 tsp cinnamon	

Nonstick cooking oil spray

- Mix the dry ingredients in a medium bowl.
- In a large bowl, whisk the egg.
- Add the other wet ingredients to the beaten egg and whisk.
- Pour the dry ingredients into the wet ingredients. Stir lightly, scraping the spoon along the edge of the bowl.
- Spray a six-muffin pan with nonstick cooking oil.
- Pour in the batter. Scrape the bowl clean with a rubber spatula.
- Bake at 350 degrees, about 20 minutes.

Six small muffins, serves 3.

Note: *This recipe uses real, honest-to-goodness **wheat bran**. It does not use raisin bran cereal.

Corn Muffins

When you stop and think about it, isn't cornbread the Bread of the Americas? The indigenous peoples of both North and South America, as well as those that came afterward, created and ate some type of cornbread. Lots of us still do, especially in the Southern U.S. Sometimes I bake Corn Muffins *for breakfast.*

Dry ingredients	**Wet ingredients**
2/3 cup cornmeal	1 egg
1/2 cup unbleached white flour	3 Tbsps canola oil
2 tsps sugar	2 Tbsps honey
1/4 tsp salt	1/2 tsp vanilla extract
	1/2 cup milk

If self-rising cornmeal: 3/4 tsp baking powder and no baking soda
If regular cornmeal: 1¼ tsp baking powder and 1/2 tsp baking soda
Nonstick cooking oil spray

- Mix the dry ingredients in a medium bowl.
- In a large bowl, whisk the egg.
- Add the other wet ingredients to the beaten egg and whisk.
- Pour the dry ingredients into the wet ingredients. Stir lightly, scraping the spoon along the edge of the bowl.
- Spray a six-muffin pan with nonstick cooking oil.
- Pour in the batter. Scrape the bowl clean with a rubber spatula.
- Bake at 350 degrees, about 20 minutes.

Six small muffins, serves 3.

Mixed Fruit Muffins

A departure from the other recipes: This one uses mostly white flour and also a little butter.

Dry ingredients
3/4 cup unbleached white flour
1/4 cup whole wheat flour
1 Tbsp sugar
1/2 tsp + 1/8 tsp baking powder
1/2 tsp baking soda
1/4 tsp salt

Wet ingredients
1 egg
2 Tbsps canola oil
1 Tbsp melted butter
2 Tbsps honey
1 tsp vanilla extract
1/2 cup milk
1/2 to 2/3 cup dried fruit combo: apricots, figs, cranberries, raisins

Nonstick cooking oil spray

- Mix the dry ingredients in a bowl.
- Whisk the wet ingredients in a separate bowl.
- Combine the dry ingredients with the wet ingredients. Stir lightly, scraping the spoon along the edge of the bowl.
- Spray a six-muffin pan with nonstick cooking oil.
- Pour in the batter. Scrape the bowl clean with a rubber spatula.
- Bake at 350 degrees, about 20 minutes.

Serves 3 or 4.

> Note: You could add 1 tablespoon of cornmeal to the batter.

Smoothies

Smoothie Talk

Smoothies can be made in an infinite number of ways. Sweet, tart, thick, thin, creamy, fruity—it's a matter of personal preference.

Keep an inventory of smoothie ingredients:
- *Refrigerator ingredients*: yogurt, milk, and juice
- *Freezer ingredients*: store-bought frozen fruit **or** fresh fruit (e.g., bananas, pineapple) that you cut up and freeze

A question. How is it possible that two people using the same recipe create two different smoothies? Some reasons I can think of:
- Fruits vary in their sugar content, size, and "frozenness."
- Blending time may vary, resulting in two different viscosities.
- It's difficult, impossible probably, to accurately measure some fruits. My recipes call for measuring *chunks* of fruit—banana, mango and pineapple—but really, how does one accurately accomplish that?

Let these smoothie recipes be a springboard for you to create your own.

Fruit Smoothies

No sugar needed—the banana provides the sweetening. These recipes are variations on a theme; some vary by only one ingredient. Sizes vary from 12 to 18 ounces. Each one has some—but never all—of these ingredients:

frozen fruit (banana, mango, strawberry, blueberry, pineapple)
frozen orange juice concentrate
apple juice
yogurt
milk

Holly's Morning Smoothie
1 frozen banana, in chunks
6 frozen strawberries
1/4 cup frozen orange juice concentrate
1/2 cup milk
1/4 cup plain yogurt

Colleen's Smoothie
1 frozen banana, in chunks
6 frozen strawberries
1/2 cup mango, in chunks
1/3 cup milk *or* **apple juice**
1/3 cup plain yogurt

Bill and Barbara's Blueberry Smoothie
1 frozen banana, in chunks
3/4 cup blueberries
1/3 cup milk
1/3 cup plain yogurt

Fruit Smoothies, Continued

Dee's Delightful Smoothie
2 frozen bananas, in chunks
1/4 cup frozen orange juice concentrate
1/4 cup milk
1/3 cup plain yogurt
Dash of ground clove and nutmeg

Fashionista Jean's Smoothie
1 frozen banana, in chunks
1/2 cup frozen pineapple, in chunks
1/3 cup blueberries
2 Tbsps frozen orange juice concentrate
1/4 cup milk
1/3 cup plain yogurt

Mountain Man Brian's Smoothie
1 frozen banana, in chunks
2/3 cup frozen mango chunks
1/3 cup blueberries
1/3 cup apple juice
1/3 cup plain yogurt

Jeep Ridin' June's Smoothie
1 frozen banana, in chunks
1/2 cup frozen pineapple, in chunks
4 frozen strawberries
1/3 cup apple juice
1/3 cup plain yogurt

Fruit Smoothies, Continued

Edgar's Smoothie
1 frozen banana, in chunks
1/2 cup frozen pineapple chunks
1/2 cup frozen mango chunks
2 Tbsps frozen orange juice concentrate
1/3 cup milk
1/3 cup yogurt

Lauri and Leigh's Smoothie
1 frozen banana
2/3 cup frozen mango chunks
4 frozen strawberries
1/3 cup apple juice
1/3 cup plain yogurt

Roberta's Smoothie
1 small frozen banana, in chunks
1 cup frozen pineapple chunks
1/3 cup milk
1/3 cup yogurt

Only two steps:
➢ Put all of the ingredients into your blender.
➢ Blend the ingredients just until the fruit is smooth.

Note: To make things easier on your blender, slightly soften frozen fruit by heating it in your microwave for a few seconds and/or slice the fruit.

Cocoa Smoothie

Chocolate!!
This recipe requires no sugar because the banana provides the sweetening.

2 Tbsps unsweetened, powdered, 100% cocoa*
2 frozen bananas, in chunks
3/4 cup milk

- Put the powdered cocoa into your blender.
- Add the banana chunks and milk.
- Blend the ingredients just until the banana is smooth. (Over-blending creates a runny smoothie.)

One 16 oz smoothie

Note: *By "cocoa" I mean unsweetened, 100% pure cocoa. It's in powder form and found in your grocery store's baking aisle.

Breakfasts

Slim Breakfast Casserole

1/2 cup already cooked meat, such as: ham, turkey bacon,
    Seasoned Ground Beef (see recipe) or leftover chicken
1¼ cups chopped potato (1 medium potato)
3 Tbsps chopped onion
3 eggs
1/4 cup milk
1 can (4 oz) Ortega chilies (optional)
1/3 cup shredded cheese
Ground cayenne pepper, to taste
Turmeric or paprika, to top
Nonstick cooking oil spray
Optional toppings: salsa, avocado, parsley or cilantro

- Dice up the meat. Set aside.
- Place the chopped potatoes and onions in a bowl with enough water to cover them and microwave for 3 to 4 minutes. Drain. Set aside.
- In a bowl, whisk eggs and milk.
- Spray non-stick cooking spray into an 8" x 8" baking dish.
- Arrange potatoes and onions in the baking dish.
- Add in egg mixture, meat, chilies, and cheese.
- Sprinkle pepper and turmeric on top.
- Bake at 350 degrees for 17 to 20 minutes, or until eggs have coagulated.
- Top with salsa, avocado, parsley or cilantro.

Serves 2.

Fried Cornmeal Mush

This dish is simple to make, but requires "an overnight stay." You cook cornmeal on your stovetop, let it cool overnight, and fry it in slices the next morning.

2½ to 3 cups water to boil
1/2 tsp salt
1 cup coarse yellow cornmeal*
1 cup cold water
1/4 cup unbleached white flour
Nonstick cooking oil spray
Optional toppings: butter, syrup, jam

The first day:
- Pour 3 cups water in pot. Add salt. Bring to a boil.
- Meanwhile, mix together cornmeal and 1 cup cold water in a small bowl.
- Slowly stir this mixture into the boiling water.
- Cook for about 10 minutes,* stirring frequently.
- Pour the mush into a small meatloaf pan or high-sided plastic container. Cool on the counter for a while. Refrigerate overnight.

The next morning:
- Pour white flour onto a dinner plate and spread it around.
- Cut a 1/2 inch slice of the hardened mush and carefully lift it out.
- Place the slice on the floured plate and dust both sides. Repeat with more slices.
- Oil skillet liberally and turn heat to medium.
- Fry your slices for a few minutes, until golden brown on each side. (Cooking time depends on how thick the slices are and how hot the skillet is.)
- Top with butter, syrup and/or jam—or enjoy it "plain."

Serves 4.

Note:*Instead of coarse grind, you can use regular grind (although I don't like its soft texture.) Boil regular grind for 5 minutes.

Jannie's Home-fried Potatoes

I cook the potatoes in a bowl of water in the microwave. Then I put the spuds in a skillet. This process produces potatoes in no time at all. And the potatoes don't stick much to the skillet.

> **1 small potato (about 1 cup when cubed)**
> **Non-stick cooking oil spray**
> **1 to 2 tsps olive oil**
> **Sage and/or basil, to taste**
> **Salt, to taste: garlic, table or seasoned**
> **Ground black pepper, to taste**
> **Paprika or turmeric, for color**
> **Cheese, any kind, to top (optional)**

- Chop potato into bite sizes.
- Place potato cubes in a bowl of water or Pyrex measuring cup and microwave for about 3 minutes.
- Meanwhile, spray nonstick cooking oil onto a skillet and turn stove to medium heat.
- With a slotted spoon, place potato cubes in the skillet and drizzle olive oil over them. Add seasonings.
- Cook on medium heat, occasionally tossing the potatoes, until the edges of the potatoes are brown, 8 to 10 minutes.
- Serve on a plate. Top with paprika or turmeric, for color, and cheese because it tastes good.

Serves 1.

Home-fries for Dawn

This recipe merely expands the previous one, Jannie's Home-Fried Potatoes. *It's also like* A Potato for Dawn *(in the Warm Vegetables section), except you don't bake a spud.*

> **1 large potato (about 1½ cup when cubed)**
> **Non-stick cooking oil spray**
> **2 tsps olive oil**
> **1 cooked sausage, any kind, such as chicken, Italian, or sage**
> **1/4 cup diced ham**
> **1/4 cup grated cheese**
> **Salt, to taste**

- Place potato cubes in a bowl of water or Pyrex measuring cup and microwave for about 3 minutes.
- Spray nonstick cooking oil onto a skillet and turn stove to medium heat.
- Drain potatoes.
- Place potatoes in the skillet and drizzle olive oil over them.
- As the potatoes cook, frequently toss them and scrape the skillet. Cook until the edges of the potatoes start to brown, 8 to 10 minutes.
- Add in sausage, ham, and cheese. Toss.
- When everything's piping hot, the spuds are ready to eat.

Serves 2.

Gringo Huevos Rancheros

This is so quick and easy you'll be eating in just a few minutes.

1 can (14 oz) chili that has both beef and beans
2 to 4 eggs
4 corn tortillas
1/4 cup shredded cheese
Salsa (optional)
Cilantro (optional)
Nonstick cooking oil spray

- Heat the chili in a sauce pan on *low* heat, stirring almost constantly.
- Spray non-stick cooking oil in a skillet and fry the eggs.
- Meanwhile wrap the tortillas in a paper towel and microwave them for about 45 seconds.
- Build "the ranch" on your plate in this order:
    - Tortillas
    - Fried eggs
    - Chili with beef and beans
    - Cheese
    - Salsa
    - Cilantro

Serves 2.

Steve's Breakfast Special

Good when you have leftover Seasoned Ground Beef *(see recipe in Beef section).*

    2 to 4 eggs
    1/2 cup *Seasoned Ground Beef* (see recipe)
    1/4 cup shredded cheese
    Salsa (optional)
    Cilantro or parsley (optional)
    Nonstick cooking oil spray

- Lightly beat eggs in a bowl.
- Heat *Seasoned Ground Beef* in the microwave for about 30 seconds.
- Spray non-stick cooking oil in a skillet and start scrambling the eggs.
- Mix in the cheese and *Seasoned Ground Beef*.
- Serve on plates. Top with salsa and cilantro or parsley.

Serves 2.

Yogurt and Fruit

You use plain yogurt and add the sweetener in yourself. That way you get a pleasant sweetness but use relatively little sweetener.

> **1/2 cup chopped berries (fresh or frozen)**
> **1/3 cup plain yogurt**
> **1/2 tsp sugar *or* 1 tsp honey**
> **1/2 tsp vanilla extract**

- Defrost the berries: the night before you eat this, measure out the frozen berries and set them in a dish in your refrigerator. (If you're using fresh berries, skip this step, of course.)
- In a bowl, fold sweetener and vanilla into the yogurt.
- Fold berries into yogurt *or* put berries in a bowl and spoon yogurt on top.

Serves 1.

San Francisco Granola

Decades ago a young woman baked granola in her huge kitchen, and I hovered over her, learning. I do not have her exact recipe, but I've developed and tested this one, and I'm naming it after the city in which I first saw granola made, the city we both loved.

Dry ingredients
1/4 cup old-fashioned oats
2 Tbsps cashews
1 Tbsp peanuts
1 Tbsp sesame seeds
1 Tbsp wheat germ
1 tsp sunflower seeds

Wet ingredients
1 Tbsp water
1 Tbsp vegetable oil
2 Tbsps honey
1/2 tsp vanilla

After baking: 1 tablespoon each of dried cranberries and raisins

- Mix the dry ingredients in a small bowl.
- Mix the wet ingredients in a medium bowl.
- Add the dry to the wet and stir.
- Spread the mixture over the entire bottom of an 8" x 8" baking dish, and scrape the bowl clean with a rubber spatula.
- Bake at 250 (two fifty) degrees for 50 to 60 minutes.
- After baking, add dried fruit.

Serves 2 to 3.

Notes:
- You can eat this dry or with milk, hot or cold. But if you eat it dry, drink a beverage because the oats may expand in your tummy.
- Use whatever kinds of nuts and seeds appeal to you in the proportions you want.

Allspice Benvenue Pancakes

This recipe is named after a street I lived on when I was in my early twenties in Berkeley. I include a story about living there in Crepes and Coyotes and Other Tales *called "The House on Benvenue."*

<u>Dry ingredients</u>	<u>Wet ingredients</u>
1/2 cup whole wheat flour	1 egg
1/4 cup unbleached white flour	1 tsp vanilla extract
1 Tbsp sugar	2/3 cup milk
2 tsps allspice	
1/2 tsp + 1/8 tsp baking powder	
1/2 tsp baking soda	
1/4 tsp salt	**Nonstick cooking oil spray**

- In a medium bowl, mix together the dry ingredients.
- In another medium bowl, lightly beat an egg.
- Add vanilla and milk to beaten egg and whisk.
- Combine wet with dry, whisking. Then stir lightly, scraping the sides with a spoon, until blended.
- Place skillet on stove, turn heat to medium-high, and spray nonstick cooking oil onto skillet.
- When skillet is sizzling hot, start making pancakes: scoop batter up with a large spoon and drop batter onto the skillet.
- Flip when done and cook the second side for a shorter amount of time than the first side.

Serves 2.

Notes:
- I use two skillets to speed up the process.
- I love the taste of whole wheat, but a little white flour gives a lighter texture.
- Tasty option: Use just 2 tablespoons of unbleached white flour (instead of 1/4 cup) and add in 2 tablespoons wheat germ.

Buckwheat Pancakes

Buckwheat flour is heavy, but that buckwheat flavor is oh-so-delicious!

Dry ingredients	**Wet ingredients**
1/2 cup buckwheat flour	1 egg
1/4 cup unbleached white flour	1 tsp vanilla extract
1 Tbsp sugar	2/3 cup milk
1/2 tsp + 1/8 tsp baking powder	
1/2 tsp baking soda	
1/2 tsp to 1 tsp cinnamon	
1/4 tsp salt	**Nonstick cooking oil spray**

- ➢ In a medium bowl, mix together the dry ingredients.
- ➢ In another medium bowl, lightly beat an egg.
- ➢ Add vanilla and milk to beaten egg and whisk.
- ➢ Combine wet with dry, whisking. Then stir lightly, scraping the sides with a spoon, until blended.
- ➢ Place skillet on stove, turn heat to medium-high, and spray nonstick cooking oil onto skillet.
- ➢ When skillet is sizzling hot, start making pancakes: scoop batter up with a large spoon and drop batter onto the skillet.
- ➢ Flip when done and cook the second side for a shorter amount of time than the first side.
- ➢ Goes good with *Cinnamon Syrup* (see recipe).

Serves 2.

> Note: Great pancakes are all about the right temperature. The skillet must be hot enough for the batter to rise, but not so hot that the pancakes burn. It's taken some practice on my part—actually, a lot of practice.

Pancakes for One

Dry ingredients
1/4 cup buckwheat flour or whole wheat flour
2 Tbsps unbleached white flour
1/2 Tbsp sugar
1/4 tsp baking powder
1/4 tsp baking soda
1/4 tsp to 1/2 tsp cinnamon *or* 1 tsp allspice *or* a combo of both
1/8 tsp salt

Wet ingredients
1 egg (smallest one in the carton)
1/2 tsp vanilla extract
1/4 cup milk

Nonstick cooking oil spray

- In a medium bowl, mix together the dry ingredients.
- In another medium bowl, lightly beat an egg.
- Add vanilla and milk to beaten egg and whisk.
- Combine wet with dry, whisking. Then stir lightly, scraping the sides with a spoon, until blended.
- Place skillet on stove, turn heat to medium-high, and spray nonstick cooking oil onto skillet.
- When skillet is sizzling hot, start making pancakes: scoop batter up with a large spoon and drop batter onto the skillet.
- Flip when done and cook the second side for a shorter amount of time than the first side.

Serves 1.

Cinnamon Syrup

You take maple syrup and jazz it up.

For 1 person
2 Tbsps pure maple syrup
1 Tbsp honey
1/8 tsp cinnamon

For 2 persons
1/4 cup pure maple syrup
2 Tbsps honey
1/4 tsp cinnamon

- Mix all ingredients in a small cup.
- Heat the cup with syrup a few seconds in your microwave.
- Spoon syrup onto your pancakes.

Crepes

When I make crepe batter I always say "That's too runny!" But stand firm and go with the liquidy batter. Vive la France!

Dry ingredients	**Wet ingredients**
2/3 cup unbleached white flour	3 eggs
2 tsps sugar	1/2 cup milk
1/8 to 1/4 tsp salt	1½ tsps vanilla extract

Nonstick cooking oil spray
Berry Syrup (see recipe) *or* **fruit spread**

Make the batter:
- Mix the dry ingredients in a bowl.
- Whisk the wet ingredients in a separate bowl.
- Add the dry ingredients to the wet ingredients and whisk until batter is smooth.

Cook the crepe:
- Spray skillet with nonstick cooking oil.*
- With one hand scoop batter with a 1/4 measuring cup and pour it into the hot skillet. Simultaneously, with your other hand grasp the skillet handle and tip the skillet around so that the batter quickly rolls around skillet, forming a very thin pancake.
- Cook crepe, then flip and cook second side. Goes fast.**

Serve the crepe:
- Spoon *Berry Syrup* or fruit spread onto the crepes.

Serves 2. Batter makes 6 thin crepes.

Notes:
* I use 2 skillets to speed up the process.
**Optional: Place the finished crepes in a 170-degree oven while you cook the other crepes.

Berry Syrup

The natural tart-and-sweetness of the fruit comes through with this recipe.

**1½ cups fresh or frozen strawberries, blueberries, blackberries,
   or a combo
2 Tbsps cornstarch
2 Tbsps cold water
1/4 cup water (to add as you heat berries)*
0 to 2 tsps sugar (Depends on how sweet or tart the fruit is.)****

- Place berries and 1 tablespoon of water into a small sauce pan. Heat on low. As the berries defrost, determine if you need to add more water.*
- Mix cornstarch and cold water in a cup. (You will probably not use all of it, but it's there just in case.)
- Just as the berry mixture begins to bubble, spoon in a little cornstarch water and stir. Mixture will thicken. Stir again.
- If syrup is too thin, add in another spoonful of cornstarch water. If it's too thick, add a spoonful of cold water. Stir. Stop when you've gotten the desired consistency.
- Taste mixture and decide if you want to add any sugar.
- Serve warm on *Crepes*, *Pancakes*, or *Blintzes* (see recipes).

Serves 2.

Notes:
*Fresh fruit needs more water than frozen as you cook the fruit.
**Strawberries are naturally gummy and tend to be sweet, and so need little cornstarch, probably no sugar. Blackberries tend to be tart; they require more sugar.

Blintzes (Filling for Crepes)

Blintzes are rolled up crepes with a rich, creamy filling.

The Filling
2/3 cup ricotta cheese*
2 to 3 tsps sugar
2 tsps vanilla extract

You'll also need
4 *Crepes* (see recipe)
Berry syrup* (see recipe) *or
Fruit spread (lemon curd, marmalade, berry preserves, fig jam, etc.)

- Mix ricotta, sugar, and vanilla in a cup. Set aside.
- When the crepes are done, spoon the ricotta mixture onto each crepe.
- Roll up the crepes. *Voila*, it's now a blintz.
- Spoon *Berry Syrup* **or** fruit spread on each blintz.

Serves 2.

Note: *You can also use any combination of ricotta, sour cream and yogurt. If so, you may need a little more sugar.

Lessons Learned

From working with Steve—and these recipes—here are some things I've learned:

- Leftovers and food inventory are good things to have. They mean less time and effort preparing a future meal.

- With just a few steps, one particular dish can easily lead to another dish.

- Be grateful that you have access to healthy food and clean water and never take those two things for granted.

- Cooking is work. It takes a certain amount of time, effort, advance planning, and experimentation to create good food.

- Cooking flops are few and far between, but they are inevitable.

- Cooking is fun, creative, and satisfying—an endeavor I whole-heartedly recommend!

Acknowledgements

Hearty and heartfelt thanks to those
that read my drafts and gave me feedback
and who believe in me and encourage me.

Family:
Mom, Jean, Brian, June, and Steve

Friends:
Andrea, Ann, Barbara, Bill, Colleen,
Dianne, Gloria, Jim, Ramona, Sherry

Cooks who inspired me:
Lauri, Leigh

Wednesday Morning Writers' Group:
Annie, Debby, Diane, Janet1, Janet2,
Kathryn, Maryellen, Sarah, Stephanie, Susana

About the Author

Janice Lynn Ross loves nature, literature, art, music, museums, history, traveling, and more. She grew up in Southern California. At age twenty, she moved to the Bay Area where she lived for three decades—as a student, preschool teacher, secretary, sales and marketing analyst, and public school elementary teacher.

Janice holds a bachelor's degree in Psychology from the University of California, Berkeley; an MBA in Marketing from Golden Gate University; and a teaching certificate from San Jose State University.

Janice is the author of *Crepes and Coyotes and Other Tales*, the companion book to this cookbook. She has also written *Like Water from a Spring: Poems, Stories, Reflections, and Pencil Scratches from a Long-Forgotten Box.*

Janice and her husband, Steve, live in Florida.

Made in the USA
Lexington, KY
07 December 2019